LECTURES ON DRYDEN

LECTURES ON DRYDEN

DELIVERED BY

A. W. VERRALL, Litt.D.

EDITED BY

MARGARET DE G. VERRALL

NEW YORK

RUSSELL & RUSSELL · INC

1963

FIRST PUBLISHED, 1914
REISSUED, 1963, BY RUSSELL & RUSSELL, INC.
BY ARRANGEMENT WITH CAMBRIDGE UNIVERSITY PRESS
L. C. CATALOG CARD NO: 63—8372

PRINTED IN THE UNITED STATES OF AMERICA

PREFACE

IN October and November 1911, Dr Verrall, as King Edward VII Professor of English Literature, delivered a course of twelve lectures on Dryden, thus carrying out the intention which he formed as soon as he was appointed to the English Chair. The reason for the selection of this subject was not only his own long-standing admiration for Dryden, but the importance of his work in the development of English prose and verse, and its comparative neglect among the younger lovers of literature at the present day. He had hoped to recast and publish in other forms—partly as essays on particular points, partly in a contemplated edition of *Absalom and Achitophel*— the material gathered for these lectures. The present volume reproduces strictly the original manuscript notes as arranged for delivery. These notes, written by himself or dictated to our daughter and to me, were unusually full, so that it has hardly been necessary to do more than give grammatical completeness to the abbreviated sentences, to alter a word here and there, and to verify or supply references.

Besides the draft used in the lecture-room, I have had before me pencilled notes made in the spring and summer of 1911, when Dr Verrall was re-reading Dryden's writings for the purposes of this course. These notes, like the full lecture-notes, were compiled solely for the lecturer's own use, and to that must be attributed some unconventionalities of expression which would not have found place in his published work. Nor would he have admitted into a work intended for readers digressions and a certain looseness of structure appropriate in the lecture-room.

Those who heard the lectures will find here some comments and suggestions the delivery of which time did not permit; in particular, I have included a lecture on *All for Love*, which was to have completed the course but which had to be omitted, as two lectures on Dryden's Religious Poems were found necessary, instead of the one originally planned. On the other hand, it is probable that many points, compressed in the notes, were more amply treated in the lectures, and there has been unavoidable curtailment where the lecturer dealt with metrical questions; for effects easily explained and illustrated by recitation to an audience do not lend themselves to reproduction in print. The proportions of the scheme have in consequence been somewhat altered; the lectures on Dryden's Odes and his verse generally fill a relatively smaller space in print than in the lecture-room, and no place has been here given to the *Secular Masque*, a reading of which, with attention to metrical effects but without other comment, concluded the course.

The general intention and purpose is apparent from the lectures themselves : they were essentially addressed to students and more particularly to Cambridge students. It was, I know, a special pleasure to my husband to have this opportunity of speaking to a Cambridge audience about a great Cambridge poet—'John Dryden of Trinity College.'

In preparing this book for publication I have received valuable assistance from friends : my thanks are due to Mr M. A. Bayfield, Mr E. H. Marsh, and more especially to Mr G. C. Macaulay, Lecturer in English in this University.

MARGARET DE G. VERRALL.

CAMBRIDGE,
   December 1913.

CONTENTS

I

DRYDEN'S WORK, CHARACTER AND INFLUENCE

Scott, in the 'Advertisement' prefixed to his complete edition of Dryden's works, writes that Dryden 'may claim at least the third place' in the list of English classics, and Gray in his *Progress of Poesy*, when he comes to English poets, celebrates Shakespeare, Milton, and Dryden. It is needless to discuss the order of merit, especially as new competitors have arisen in the nineteenth century. These have not yet been sifted; even if the two great Poets Laureate of last century, Wordsworth and Tennyson, obtain two hundred years—and perhaps they will not obtain more—of permanent interest, their work can hardly be of higher value than that of Dryden.

Gray's words in the *Progress of Poesy* are carefully chosen. Passing on from Milton, he writes of Dryden's 'less presumptuous car' borne 'wide o'er the fields of glory.' 'Wide' serves to remind us of Dryden's success in almost every class of literature. In drama he was the principal figure from the Restoration to the Revolution, prolific both in comedy and tragedy; the heroic play, of which his writings are the leading examples, was at one time supposed to have rivalled the works of the Jacobean playwrights.

Then he became the voice of the nation in a supreme political crisis, and created for this purpose almost a new type of poem, akin to satire but essentially different—the First Part of *Absalom and Achitophel*, published in November, 1681.

From this there was a double development, first in the direction of personal satire, where the result was *The Medal* (March, 1682), *Mac Flecknoe* (October, 1682), and the satire on Settle and Shadwell, as Doeg and Og, in the Second Part of *Absalom and Achitophel*, published in November, 1682. These poems were not original in form, but unprecedented in smartness, in energy, and in eloquence.

The second development lay in the direction of arguments on religion, then a part of politics. Here Dryden represented the national voice in a form practically new and characterised by dexterity and apparent simplicity. He takes the tone of the reasonable man, who tries to see his way amid the difficulties of the subject; he commands an extra-ordinary range of feeling, from the highest passion to mere conversation, but the transitions from one mood to another are perfectly natural and the whole is written in almost faultless verse. The two poems, *Religio Laici* (November, 1682) and *The Hind and the Panther* (April, 1687) represent opposite sides, the latter poem having been published after his conversion in the reign of James II.

Then again take his narrative poetry. Here lay his ambition; the English epic, then and still wanting,—for Milton's *Paradise Lost* is not a national epic—he never achieved, but he won notable successes in this line. In his early career, during the interruption of his dramatic work occasioned by his absence from London at the time of the Great Plague, he wrote *Annus Mirabilis*, 1666. This poem, which describes the Dutch wars and the Fire of London, is not an epic but is an essay in that direction, as Dryden himself clearly recognised; this he shows by his judgements upon the Latin epic poets, especially Lucan and Virgil, in the *Letter to Sir R. Howard* prefixed to the poem. The work is not really Virgilian, but Dryden's comparison of it with the Roman national epic is all the more significant, as showing that he conceived the object as similar. Dryden's poem contains much admirable work and is still interesting. He was led back to narrative poetry in his closing years by his straitened circumstances after the Revolution. He turned then to translation and adaptation of other poets; with assistance, he translated the whole of Virgil, a work which was almost a national monument. But its success has been overrated; Pope, for instance, called it 'the most noble and spirited translation which he knew in any language,' a judgement which we cannot endorse. He also translated or adapted parts of Chaucer and of Ovid and made poetical adaptations from the prose of Boccaccio. His Chaucerian translations were admirable and new to the public ; specially to be recommended to readers are his versions of *Palamon and Arcite* and *The Cock and the Fox*. The stories, fables as he calls them, based on Boccaccio are virtually original. Take for instance *Theodore and Honoria* : Boccaccio's tale is neither a poem nor a poetic story ; Dryden's version could hardly be improved. This is a great effect to be produced by an old man near seventy, already at the height of his fame and not expected to succeed in this way.

Then, to turn to lyric poetry : the songs in the plays and a few other pieces show his admirable ear ; he wrote simple rhythms with a new perfection. But here again there was a surprise at the end. The complicated lyric with irregular metre—the ode—had been practised by Dryden to a small extent, it is true, but beyond the common standard ; then, happily using casual occasions—the meetings of a musical society—he gave to the ode and to lyric verse generally an entirely new standard of technical execution. The two *Odes for St Cecilia's Day*, 1687 and 1697, are immensely important both technically and historically : from them derives the work in this line of Gray, Collins, Coleridge, Wordsworth, and Tennyson. The second ode, *Alexander's Feast, or the Power of Music*, with its characteristic combination of simplicity and science is almost unrivalled in popularity :—' None but the brave deserves the fair,' and ' like another Helen fired another Troy,' are familiar to many who have never opened a volume containing Dryden's 'Works.' This ode was written when Dryden was in his sixty-seventh year.

Beyond this, there is much work not easily classed, but taking the form of complimentary pieces, addresses, epistles, etc. The poem conveying to Lady Castlemaine Dryden's thanks for her patronage of an unsuccessful play in 1663 is important as giving perhaps the first decisive proof of his special power. This series of poems also ends only with his life and rises to the last, in the domestic and autobiographical Epistle to his cousin John Driden, a rural magistrate and member of Parliament. This Epistle was included in the last of Dryden's published volumes, which contained among other matter the translations from Chaucer; the Epistle was very popular at the time and is still pleasing. It is Horatian, more so than the Epistles of Pope, for like the Roman poet's writing it excites a friendly feeling in the reader.

Further, there is a large mass of prose, mostly connected with the poetry, in the form of critical prefaces—very characteristic of Dryden, who was a conscious artist—but some similar work was independently published. Most worth study are perhaps the *Essay of Dramatic Poesy*, written in 1668, and the *Preface to the Fables* in 1700. His style is pleasant and gentlemanly, and his work takes an important place in the development of practicable prose. In the period in which he wrote England saw the first formation of a large literary society in London, and this is reflected in his dedications; the courtly profusion of compliment is characteristic of the age but is managed by Dryden with singular dignity.

More might be added, but this is sufficient to prove the accuracy of Gray's descriptive 'wide.' Even if we make all possible deductions, such for instance as the whole of the dramatic work—an exception which is, however, not fair, for the play of *All for Love* certainly has merit—the permanent part still remains very large, when the lapse of time is considered. The indestructible part of Dryden's work is sufficient for a first-rate reputation; the First Part of *Absalom and Achitophel, Theodore and Honoria*, and the two *Odes for St Cecilia's Day*, are more than enough in themselves.

The historical interest of Dryden to a student of English literature is immense. He was the principal figure and agent in the formation of permanent standard English, the conscious work of the age. In this his action was perfectly deliberate; he intended to improve the literature and especially the poetry of his time, to improve it generally, that is to say, and to raise the normal standard. In his *Threnodia Augustalis*, a lament on the death of Charles II, he gives us a literary retrospect describing how the muses return with the King :—

> And such a plenteous crop they bore
> Of *purest* and *well-winnow'd* grain
> As Britain never saw before ;

and the same feeling is expressed in the *Epistle to Sir Robert Howard.* To understand the precise meaning of this claim on behalf of the Post-Restoration poetry we had better take an instance.

Cowley, a predecessor of Dryden, writing in the reign of Charles I, was a man of thorough academic training—he had been educated here at Trinity College—a poet of high reputation and ambitious of style. He was the creator of the 'Pindaric Art' and in his *Ode in Praise of Pindar*, where sublimity is contrasted with simplicity of style, there are fine lines. He describes Pindar's poetry which 'Like a swoln flood from some steep mountain pours along'; and writes that 'The grave can but the dross of him devour.' And yet Cowley can admit the following :—

> Whether some brave young man's untimely fate
> In words worth dying for he celebrate,
>   Such mournful and such pleasing words
> *As joy to his mother's and his mistress' grief affords*;
>   He bids him live and grow in fame,
>   Among the stars he *sticks* his name.

The verse 'as joy to his mother's and his mistress' grief affords' has almost as many mistakes as words: the forced grammar of 'affords' is especially offensive in the rhyming word; the emphasis of the rhyme falls upon a weak word, and that word the wrong word, for 'gives' or 'brings,' not 'affords,' represents the meaning; there is a faulty omission of the second 'to' in 'to his mother's and his mistress'' so that it would be supposed that only one person was indicated ; the word 'his' is lopped, 'to 's mother's and 's mistress' ' ; there is a clumsy inversion of the whole sentence, the word 'joy' being apparently the subject whereas it is found ultimately to be the object of the verb. So again in the last line quoted the word 'sticks' is at least unlucky, even if we suppose it to have been unobjectionable at the time.

This case is typical ; there is a very small amount of composition earlier than the Restoration which is not open to like objections. This was the chaff which Dryden justly desired to 'winnow,' and this object he achieved ; such lapses as Cowley's are hardly possible in a poet of reputation since Dryden's time.

The deliberate attempt to improve English literary style was part of a movement natural in the circumstances of the time. The increase of wealth and the diffusion of culture, together with the growth of London, brought together a large but yet coherent society. There was also the example of France, where the Academy had been founded in 1635, and where the Court of Louis XIV was the centre of French classical literature. England was much in arrear ; there was no authorised grammar, no dictionary. Dryden himself wanted an Academy ; but the whole movement of the age was academic.

The appearance of Dryden at this time was fortunate. His practical command of English is immense ; so too is his vigour, of which the main principle is that there is no waste, no 'chaff.' There is hardly an idle word ; the metrical emphasis is correctly adapted to the meaning, there are no 'fetches' for rhyme, and his instinct for vocabulary, for the permanent, accounts for the astonishing freshness of his composition; there is almost nothing in his writing which marks a date. No doubt this is partly the consequence of subsequent imitation, and of the adoption of Dryden by later writers as a standard; Charles Fox, for instance, told Lord Holland that he would admit no word into his book, his projected *History of James II*, for which he had not the authority of Dryden. But this is not sufficient explanation, and does not extend to his grammar or to the turning of his phrases. The point is best illustrated by examples from his writing.

Let us take first the *Song* from the play *An Evening's Love*, published in 1668 :—

Damon.   Celimena, of my heart
            None shall e'er bereave you :
            If, with your good leave, I may
            Quarrel with you once a day,
            I will never leave you.

Celimena.   Passion's but an empty name,
            Where respect is wanting :
            Damon, you mistake your aim ;
            Hang your heart, and burn your flame,
            If you must be ranting.

Damon.   Love as dull and muddy is
            As decaying liquor :
            Anger sets it on the lees,
            And refines it by degrees,
            Till it works the quicker.

Celimena. Love by quarrels to beget
　　　　　Wisely you endeavour;
　　　　　With a grave physician's wit,
　　　　　Who, to cure an ague fit,
　　　　　Put me in a fever.

Damon. Anger rouses love to fight,
　　　　　And his only bait is,
　　　　　'Tis the spur to dull delight,
　　　　　And is but an eager bite,
　　　　　When desire at height is.

Celimena. If such drops of heat can fall
　　　　　In our wooing weather;
　　　　　If such drops of heat can fall,
　　　　　We shall have the devil and all
　　　　　When we come together.

Or again take the Jacobites' Song, *The Beautiful
Lady of the May*, written probably in 1691, and
published after Dryden's death :—

A quire of bright beauties in spring did appear,
To choose a May-lady to govern the year;
All the nymphs were in white, and the shepherds in green,
The garland was given, and Phillis was queen;
But Phillis refus'd it; and sighing did say,
'I'll not wear a garland while Pan is away.'

While Pan and fair Syrinx are fled from our shore,
The Graces are banish'd, and Love is no more:
The soft god of pleasure that warm'd our desires
Has broken his bow, and extinguish'd his fires,
And vows that himself and his mother will mourn,
Till Pan and fair Syrinx in triumph return.

Forbear your addresses, and court us no more,
For we will perform what the Deity swore:
But, if you dare think of deserving our charms,
Away with your sheephooks, and take to your arms;

Then laurels and myrtles your brows shall adorn,
When Pan and his son and fair Syrinx return.

Instances might be multiplied indefinitely. Let us take as an example in prose a passage from the *Epistle to the Whigs*, the introduction to the satire *The Medal*. The Epistle is throughout a furious invective, the most dangerous of moods and the most rapidly out of date ; yet Dryden both achieves his force without exceeding in point of language the range of normal speech, and also by some instinct keeps so close to the genius of English that he might almost have written yesterday. The language is much more normal and modern, for instance, than that of Junius, some ninety years later :—

> But I would ask you one civil question : What right has any man among you, or any association of men (to come nearer to you) who out of parliament cannot be considered in a public capacity, to meet, as you daily do, in factious clubs, to vilify the government in your discourses, and to libel it in all your writings? Who made you judges in Israel? Or how is it consistent with your zeal of the public welfare to promote sedition? Does your definition of loyal, which is to serve the King according to the laws, allow you the license of traducing the executive power with which you own he is invested? You complain that his Majesty has lost the love and confidence of his people ; and by your very urging it you endeavour what in you lies to make him lose them. All good subjects abhor the thought of arbitrary power, whether it be in one or many : if you were the patriots you would seem, you would not at this rate incense the multitude to assume it ; for no sober man can fear it, either from the King's disposition or his practice, or, even where you would odiously lay it, from his Ministers. Give us leave to enjoy the government and the benefit of laws

under which we were born, and which we desire to transmit to our posterity. You are not the trustees of the public liberty : and if you have not right to petition in a crowd, much less have you to intermeddle in the management of affairs, or to arraign what you do not like, which in effect is everything that is done by the King and Council. Can you imagine that any reasonable man will believe you respect the person of his Majesty, when 'tis apparent that your seditious pamphlets are stuffed with particular reflections on him ? If you have the confidence to deny this, 'tis easy to be evinced from a thousand passages, which I only forbear to quote, because I desire they should die and be forgotten.

Or take the following passage from *The Medal* itself (123 ff.). In this there is one archaism, 'brave' for 'bravo,' a point instantly noted by the reader of the present day—and this in the case of a poet more than 200 years old :—

> Too happy England, if our good we knew,
> Would we possess the freedom we pursue !
> The lavish government can give no more ;
> Yet we repine, and plenty makes us poor.
> God tried us once ; our rebel fathers fought ;
> He glutted them with all the power they sought,
> Till, master'd by their own usurping brave,
> The free-born subject sunk into a slave.
> We loathe our manna, and we long for quails ;
> Ah ! what is man, when his own wish prevails !
> How rash, how swift to plunge himself in ill,
> Proud of his power and boundless in his will !

The life of Dryden is easily accessible, in Scott's complete edition of Dryden's works, in Professor Saintsbury's *Life* in the series of *English Men of Letters* (edited by Lord Morley), or in Christie's

Memoir in the Globe Edition of Dryden's *Poetical Works*. Here therefore I note only some aspects of importance.

Dryden's native rank was neither too high nor too low; he was essentially a gentleman in the proper sense of the word—born, that is, and bred and placed with natural access to the more polished part of society. He was the son of a country gentleman of good family, in succession to a baronetcy; Dryden's own son succeeded to the title after his father's death, and there was another baronetcy on the side of Dryden's mother, Mary Pickering. John Dryden was a King's Scholar at Westminster, and a Westminster Scholar at Trinity College, Cambridge. The important part of his school days coincided with the Civil War, and his University course with the Usurpation, for he stayed at Cambridge from 1650 to 1657. One poem, *Upon the Death of the Lord Hastings*, written while he was at Westminster, is among his published works, but it is not good. Of his University course we do not know much; there is a record that he was punished in his second year for contumacy to the Vice-Master, but as he took his B.A. degree at the usual date he apparently did not waste his time here. He stayed in Cambridge seven years, that being then the usual length of the course for Orders in the Church of England, but he did not take Orders, nor proceed to his M.A. degree. There is a grateful allusion to Trinity College in his *Life of Plutarch* : ' I particularly observed [this passage] when I read

Plutarch in the library of Trinity College, in
Cambridge, to which foundation I gratefully ac-
knowledge a great part of my education.' This
allusion, written in 1683, is better evidence of
Dryden's real feeling than the often quoted passage
from the *Prologue to the University of Oxford*,
printed in 1684 and probably delivered at Oxford
in 1681 :—

> Oxford to him a dearer name shall be
> Than his own mother-university.
> Thebes did his green unknowing youth engage ;
> He chooses Athens in his riper age.

For it must never be forgotten, in judging of
Dryden's sentiments, that he wrote strictly for the
occasion ; this Prologue was directly addressed to
the University of Oxford, and in a private letter we
find him saying, in connexion with another Prologue
and Epilogue to be spoken at Oxford : 'how easy
'tis to pass anything upon an university, and how
gross flattery the learned will endure.'

Dryden's family politics were Parliamentarian ;
there was little fortune, barely a subsistence for the
eldest son. John Dryden apparently settled in
London about the year 1657 and worked there for
a bookseller. There is no suggestion of a severe
struggle for livelihood, and he does not seem to
have lost touch with society, if we may judge by his
rapid success after the Restoration. Not long after
his coming to London we find him on intimate terms
with a son of the Earl of Berkshire, Sir Robert
Howard, a poet and dramatist. Dryden's enemies

brought against him a charge of sponging on Howard, and we have Dryden's own statement in the letter prefixed to *Annus Mirabilis* that he was 'many ways obliged to' Sir Robert, who had 'not only been careful of' his fortune, but solicitous for his reputation. There is no sufficient evidence on the point to make judgement possible.

In 1663 he married Sir Robert's sister, Lady Elizabeth Howard, and his enemies accounted for the marriage by bringing charges of indiscretion against the lady. No special explanation, however, seems necessary. Dryden was already in some favour at Court, as is shown by the patronage of Lady Castlemaine and the tone of his address to her. We have a later picture of himself and his associates about the year 1667, in his *Essay of Dramatic Poesy*, and there is also evidence of good relations with his wife's family, for, during his absence from London at the time of the plague, he resided at Charlton in Wiltshire, the property of the Earl of Berkshire. His family consisted of three sons. There was much contemporary gossip about his family relations but nothing is really known; there was no known breach with his wife, and his own letters, among other things, show evidence of strong affection for his children. The argument that his marriage was unhappy, drawn from uncomplimentary allusions to marriage in his works, is futile; the insanity, in old age, of Lady Elizabeth is nothing to the purpose; some evidence of his actual views on marriage may be derived from his *Epistle to John*

Driden, himself a bachelor. Here, after strong
language on the perils of marriage, he adds :—

> Not that my verse would blemish all the fair ;
> But yet, if some be bad, 'tis wisdom to beware,
> And better shun the bait than struggle in the snare.
> Thus have you shunn'd and shun the married state,
> Trusting as little as you can to Fate.

These lines, written after some thirty-five years of
marriage, may surely in fairness be considered to
include his own case as at least tolerable, and
being contained in the Epistle to his cousin John
Driden, which is largely autobiographical and
entirely personal, they outweigh many gibes in the
comedies, in which there is no reason to see a
personal intention. The allusion to marriage in this
Epistle is not quoted, so far as I am aware, by any
of Dryden's biographers, but seems to deserve
attention from those who are interested in the
question of his personal relations.

Dryden's connexion with the Court after the
Restoration has been attributed to abandonment of
principle, and in support of this view his accusers
quote the stanzas *To the Memory of Oliver Cromwell.*
But, as we shall see when we discuss this poem[1],
there is no evidence there for his approval of military
despotism. At the Restoration no doubt, as on other
occasions, Dryden went with the stream. He was
poor for his position. The Poet Laureateship, con-
ferred on him in 1670, brought him £200 a year,
and to this was added later another pension of £100

---

[1] See below, p. 92.

a year. But his salary was ill paid, and remunerative work was necessary to him. This the theatre provided, and his main work during twenty years was for the stage. This was unfortunate, as he knew himself, for he had hardly any real dramatic power; he could make situations but not characters, and the characters that he describes can never be really pictured. Further, the coarseness of the stage encouraged Dryden's worst tendency, and infected other work, such as his songs, and even the opening lines of *Absalom and Achitophel*. (This subject I shall ignore as far as possible.) Other work also he did for money: ' Poets subsist not but by favour of sovereign princes and great men '; hence his dedications, his complimentary addresses, puffs, and prologues. What is extant in this kind is not voluminous and the rate of profit is uncertain; he is said, for instance, but not on unimpeachable authority, to have received five hundred guineas for *Eleonora*, ' a panegyrical poem dedicated to the memory of the late Countess of Abingdon,' a lady with whom he was not personally acquainted.

Even with all allowance for the convention and feeling of the day, Dryden's was not a dignified position, but Macaulay's words, ' a life of mendicancy and adulation,' are much too strong. Dryden dispenses his compliments like a patron, and of mendicancy there is no evidence whatever. It is true that he pressed the Government for a further endowment to set him free for the epic he wished to write, and that he specially urged this after *Absalom and Achitophel* had given him some claim upon the Government ; but this is not 'mendicancy.'

After the Revolution Dryden was in great straits of poverty, from which he was rescued by friends and in particular by the Earl of Dorset.   To Dorset, to whom the Essay on Satire preceding the translations from Juvenal was addressed in 1693, strong expressions of gratitude are employed both in that Essay and in private letters : ' May the Almighty God return it for me, both in blessing you here, and rewarding you hereafter,' but there is no proof of unwarranted solicitation on Dryden's part.   He was no hero in his pecuniary relations, or indeed in any others.   Milton might have written his epic on the income that Dryden had, perhaps even on the diminished income which he had after the Revolution ; but no one is bound to be Milton.   And, whatever our judgement on the ethical point, at all events we must recognise that Dryden's position between a literary Court and the literary class was eminently favourable for a polisher of language.

As to his opinions, he had no profound or coherent theory in politics, in religion, or even in criticism.   He has been praised for his arguments, and justly praised ; in a certain sense it is true that, as he wrote himself, ' they cannot be good poets who are not accustomed to argue well.' His logic made him clear and his controversial tone increased his vigour, but the logic is of the moment; arguments for a given position are readily found and well put, but there is no system, not even in the matter of literary criticism.

In politics Dryden was a 'King's man'—the word Tory did not come into use till after 1679. He held that the history of the past usurpation had proved the practical necessity of monarchy, of a limited monarchy, to the preservation of a free constitution, and he was determined not at any price to repeat the story of 1642–1659. But this is quite different from the Tory as he is apt to be painted by Whig historians. Dryden has no superstition about hereditary monarchy. He founds himself, not upon 'divine right' but upon the action of 'our fathers' and on practical experience. Thus, in *The Medal*, he writes of 'our fathers':—

> Who, to destroy the seeds of civil war,
> Inherent right in monarchs did declare;
> And, that a lawful power might never cease,
> Secur'd succession to secure our peace.

Nor had he any religious feeling : he cannot be called an Anglican, except perhaps for a few years after 1681 ; but at no time had he any superstition about non-resistance. His language in referring to the Civil War is easily misapprehended if we do not note his reticences and allow for the difficulty of his position ; he condemns the Civil War generally in terms which, inconsiderately construed, might seem to cover approval of submission to the Star Chamber and the imposition of Ship Money. But no such approval nor any word in favour of arbitrary power, whether in Charles I or Cromwell, will be found in his writings, and on the contrary his pride in his ancestors' resistance to arbitrary taxation comes

out strongly in his Epistle to his cousin John
Driden :—

> Patriots in peace assert the people's right,
> With noble stubbornness resisting might :
> No lawless mandates from the court receive,
> Nor lend by force, but in a body give.
> Such was your generous grandsire, free to grant
> In parliaments that weigh'd their Prince's want :
> But so tenacious of the common cause
> As not to lend the king against his laws ;
> And, in a loathsome dungeon doom'd to lie,
> In bonds retain'd his birth-right liberty,
> And sham'd oppression, till it set him free.

There is no fair ground for doubt that such were
always his sentiments ; even in the poems of the
early Restoration, *Astraea Redux* and the *Poem on
the Coronation of Charles II*, we note the remarkable
absence of any praise of Charles I.   It is so almost
everywhere ; the introduction of the phrase ' King
Charles the Martyr' in the preface to *Religio Laici*
startles an accustomed reader of Dryden, and is
obviously adopted for the special occasion in order
to give the Anglican tone.   Nor indeed does the
description of Charles I as a 'martyr' import a
general political approval of his conduct.

The destruction of the monarchy was passionately
disapproved by Dryden, and he regarded the exile
of Charles II as a fatal injustice.   How it should
have been avoided he does not say, and did not
know, but this does not make his theoretical position
untenable ; it was doubtless that of thousands of his
contemporaries.   As a critic of statesmen and policies

he was not consistent. He was indeed no politician, except as a poet at the time of the singular conjunction of the year 1681. Generally speaking he was inclined to think the King's policy right, and therefore approved of the Triple Alliance in 1668, and of the Dutch War of 1672. In his subsequent criticism of Shaftesbury and others, he forgets or ignores his own fluctuations—not an uncommon or an unpardonable sin.

Absalom and Achitophel was the natural and singularly happy outcome of his creed and habits. A King's man had his opportunity at this crisis, for undoubtedly in 1680 the King and his supporters averted a ghastly catastrophe. Dryden was at this moment prepared, spiritually and technically, and the result was the finest political poem that exists. Christie, it should be noted, attempts in his *Memoir of Dryden*, prefixed to the Globe Edition of Dryden's Poems, to show that *Absalom and Achitophel* is merely one turn in a course without principles, and that Dryden's opposition to Shaftesbury and the Exclusionists was a sudden and arbitrary move to recover ground with the King after supposed slackness or disaffection. For this view I can see no evidence at all; caprice, dictated by partiality for Shaftesbury, would seem to account for much in Christie's *Memoir*. The political situation of 1681 and Dryden's sentiments are best considered when we come to discuss *Absalom and Achitophel* in detail[1].

[1] See below, p. 49.

So too Dryden's religious opinions will better be discussed in connexion with his religious poems, or rather his poems of religious politics, *Religio Laici* and *The Hind and the Panther.* Was his conversion to Roman Catholicism, between the dates of these two poems, sincere ?   This is a chief point of controversy for his biographers, and is not without literary interest ; for if there is no reality in his conversion, there is none in his religion.   Both poems are then grossly hypocritical and such a view must affect our taste of them.   Macaulay said of Dryden that he 'knew little and cared little about religion' ; 'knew little' is true, but 'cared little' is not quite true, at least not after the year 1680, when he was approaching his fiftieth year.   To a careful observer, Dryden's conversion, whether genuine or not, should be no surprise.

To turn to his critical opinions : he had a sound instinct and taste for good things, for Shakespeare, for instance, and for Milton.   Expressions of his admiration for Shakespeare are frequent in his critical writings ; the best known is perhaps that in the *Essay of Dramatic Poesy* :—

> Shakespeare was the man who of all modern, and perhaps ancient poets, had the largest and most comprehensive soul. All the images of Nature were still present to him, and he drew them, not laboriously, but luckily ; when he describes anything, you more than see it, you feel it too.   Those who accuse him to have wanted learning, give him the greater commendation : he was naturally learned ; he needed not the spectacles of books to read Nature ; he looked inwards, and found her there.

Dryden had an early and enthusiastic admiration for *Paradise Lost* and there is evidence of his close study of Milton's early works, not only indirectly in his own *Song for St Cecilia's Day*[1] but also directly in his criticism of Milton's rhymed work in the *Discourse concerning the Original and Progress of Satire* :—

> Rhyme was not his talent; he had neither the ease of doing it, nor the graces of it; which is manifest in his *Juvenilia*, or verses written in his youth, where his rhyme is always constrained and forced, and comes hardly from him, at an age when the soul is most pliant, and the passion of love makes almost every man a rhymer, though not a poet.

Modern criticism will not adopt all that Dryden says in the above passage. He was offended by the laxness of structure in the early poems and also by the not infrequent false emphasis on the rhyming word produced by an otherwise purposeless inversion; as, for instance, the 'mantle *blue*' in *Lycidas*. He differed from Milton on the desirability of using rhyme in epic poetry, but neither this disagreement nor his disapproval of Milton as a rhymer checked his admiration, any more than did their differences in politics or in religion. For Chaucer he had a thorough appreciation, and a natural affinity with him, as he himself recognised; writing, in the *Preface to the Fables*, of his translation of Chaucer's work, he says : 'I found (if I may be permitted to say it of myself) I had a soul congenial to his, and that I had been conversant in the same studies.'

[1] See below, p. 185.

But in his literary views, as in other matters, Dryden had no system. He sometimes changed sides, as on the question of the use of rhyme in drama, and was always eager for the opinion which for the moment he held. Throughout these variations he is always characterised by strong common sense. He felt his way to improvements of practice, making rules and theory twist as they must.

He was a good Latinist, well read in the Latin orators and poets, from whom he learnt compactness and force. His history of literature, on the other hand, is second-hand and not trustworthy, and he had not much Greek, then a speciality. He translated the first book of the *Iliad*, it is true, and wrote a Life of Plutarch; but this proves nothing as to his scholarship in Greek. He seldom touches on Greek literature and never shows more than a second-hand acquaintance with it. His curious struggles over the 'Unities' I propose to discuss at length later on[1]; the struggles and errors are of interest as illustrating the general position of criticism at the time.

In estimating Dryden it cannot be forgotten that he sacrificed, at least on one occasion, judgement to convenience: his horrible treatment of Shakespeare's play of *The Tempest* cannot represent his better mind.

His character was kindly; he was fond of society, but diffident with his superiors, and not a pushing man. The description of him given by Congreve,

---

[1] See below, p. 117 ff.

the friend of his old age, is much better evidence of this aspect of his character than any that can be produced on the other side, and Congreve's account is confirmed by the general tone of his dedications, addresses, and so on. As regards his private conduct, he was certainly no model, but he gave no scandal, and even in that age, when scandal was not easily given, to avoid it meant something. Bishop Burnet called him 'a monster of immodesty and impurity of all sorts,' but Burnet was no fair witness and even this phrase may be explained—and was so explained by Burnet's son—as referring not to Dryden's private character but to his plays. Even the contemporary lampooners alleged nothing notable against him. We may accept with confidence Congreve's words: 'Indeed Mr Dryden had personal qualities to challenge both love and esteem from all who were truly acquainted with him.'

II

THE EPISTLES

THE interest of Dryden's so-called *Epistles* lies in the consideration of them as a series showing the development of his literary skill. They cover a period of nearly fifty years, from the Epistle to John Hoddesdon, written in 1650, to the Epistle to the poet's cousin, John Driden, written at the end of 1699.

The name 'Epistle' is taken from Horace, but there is no agreement except in name between the Epistles of Horace and of Dryden; the form of a letter, regular in Horace, is rare with Dryden. Only one of Dryden's, the letter to Sir George Etherege, minister at Ratisbon, has the strict epistolary form; the others are Addresses in verse on a particular, often a literary, occasion. A similar use of the word 'Epistle' to describe an address or dedication is found in Dryden's prose *Epistle to the Whigs*, accompanying his satire *The Medal*. These addresses in fact, generally in praise of a book and published with it, correspond with our modern press-notices, and some of them have a strong resemblance to 'log-rolling.' Thus Dryden's

Epistle to Lee on his play of *The Rival Queens*, published in 1677, was a reply to Lee's complimentary verses to Dryden prefixed to *The State of Innocence*, and the situation is fully recognised in Dryden's opening lines. To put the matter briefly, we may say that many of these 'Epistles' were in fact an advertisement of the volumes to which they were prefixed.

Not all deserve comment, but an examination in chronological sequence is not without value to the student of Dryden.

The first is addressed 'To John Hoddesdon, On his Divine Epigrams,' and was prefixed to a volume of religious verse, called *Sion and Parnassus*, written by a young man of eighteen, the 'Epigrams' being on various texts of the Bible. The book was published in 1650, when Dryden himself was about eighteen, and he is described in it as J. Dryden of Trinity College. In criticising the metrical technique of his verses it is interesting to remember that at a later period Dryden declared that metrical technique was not possible for the young. In some lines to the memory of Oldham, who died in 1683, aged about 30, Dryden writes :—

> O early ripe! to thy abundant store
> What could advancing age have added more?
> It might (what nature never gives the young)
> Have taught the numbers of thy native tongue.

as if early work were generally deficient in metre. This is in fact not true, but Dryden, we must not forget, is always apt to speak for the occasion, and his sentiments however strongly expressed often represent but a momentary feeling. Pope will readily occur to us as an instance of early metrical skill, and much of Shakespeare's work was written before he was thirty. Not only therefore is Dryden's opinion not true of youthful poets in general, but skill in manipulation of verse is really characteristic of the period at which he was then writing, when there was a general diffusion of metrical knowledge and training of the ear. Even Dryden's statement, in the *Essay of Dramatic Poesy*, that 'the sweetness of English verse was never understood or practised' before the time of Waller, Denham, and their contemporaries is false, unless we interpret his words in the sense of 'not generally appreciated.' Dryden himself at the age of eighteen was thoroughly trained, and, as this poem shows, wrote, not as a boy does, but as men generally write.

There is however plenty to criticise in the poem: take the first 16 lines :—

> Thou hast inspir'd me with thy soul, and I,
> Who ne'er before could ken of poetry,
> Am grown so good proficient I can lend
> A line in commendation of my friend.
> Yet 'tis but of the second hand; if aught
> There be in this, 'tis from thy fancy brought.
> Good thief who darest, Prometheus-like, aspire,
> And fill thy poems with celestial fire,
> Enliven'd by these sparks divine, their rays
> Add a bright lustre to thy crown of bays.
> Young eaglet, who thy nest thus soon forsook,
> So lofty and divine a course hast took

As all admire, before the down begin
To peep as yet upon thy smoother chin;
And, making Heaven thy aim, hast had the grace
To look the Sun of Righteousness in the face.

The general defects may be thus summarised :

(1) There is no correspondence between the form and the sense. Thus the sense of the first four lines is, 'after reading your epigrams, I, who could not even form an opinion on poetry, can now actually state my opinion in poetical shape,' whereas the verse-form throws the emphasis upon '*lend*'— 'lend A line in commendation of my friend.'

(2) The rhyme is often forced, a danger later recognised by Dryden, both in the Preface to *Annus Mirabilis*, where he says that verses made for the sake of rhyme were practised by 'our fathers,' and again in the *Essay of Dramatic Poesy*, where he tells us that 'some writers yet living...first taught us...to make our rhyme so properly a part of the verse, that it should never mislead the sense, but itself be led and governed by it.' Obviously in the last line but one of the above-quoted passage 'the grace' falls under Dryden's own condemnation.

(3) There is a neglect of 'quantity,' that is of the weight of syllables. In the *Essay of Dramatic Poesy*, written in 1668, nearly twenty years after the lines to Hoddesdon, Dryden expressly declares this neglect of syllabic weight legitimate; any dissyllable, he says, makes a good foot of ordinary modern verse. But his later practice does not conform with this theory, and we do not long continue to find

in his work such neglect of syllabic weight as in
the following :—

> *Enliven'd by* these sparks divine, *their rays,*
> —*' thus soon,'*—*' hast took,'*—
> May learn to *make like* in *just praise* of thee.

(4) There is a loose accumulation of images—
or 'conceits'; 'rays' add lustre to 'bays,' and
Hoddesdon is not only 'Prometheus-like,' but he
is an 'eaglet,' with as yet no 'down' upon his
'chin.'

On the other hand we have a good line in
v. 10:—

> Add a bright lustre to thy crown of bays.

The sentiment of the poem is characteristic of
Dryden ; there is no real religion in it, no awe.
How else could he write :—

> Thou hast commenc'd betimes a saint ; go on,
> Mingling diviner streams with Helicon,
> That they who view what Epigrams here be,
> May learn to make like, in just praise of thee.

Clearly Dryden's interest was in 'Helicon' and not
in the 'diviner streams.'

The next Epistle, written in 1660, and addressed
to Sir Robert Howard, who three years afterwards
became Dryden's brother-in-law, was prefixed to a
volume of Howard's poems, containing among other
things translations of the *Achilleis* of Statius, and
of the Fourth Book of the *Aeneid.* The praise is
indiscriminate ; Howard has improved both Statius
and Virgil ! But the figures are managed better—

Howard himself is praised for his moderation in metaphor—and the quantity and rhyme are in places correct, according to the standard of Dryden's later versification :—

> Or is it Fortune's work, that in your head
> The curious net that is for fancies spread
> Lets through its meshes every meaner thought,
> While rich ideas there are only caught?
> Sure that's not all; this is a piece too fair
> To be the child of chance, and not of care.
> No atoms casually together hurl'd
> Could e'er produce so beautiful a world;
> Nor dare I such a doctrine here admit
> As would destroy the providence of wit.

These lines are characteristic both of Dryden's interest in the science of his day—*rete mirabile* was the name of the network of blood-vessels at the base of the brain—and of his irreverent handling of theology.

At the end of 1662, or early in 1663, Dryden prefixed a poem to a book in which Dr Charleton propounded a theory about the building of Stonehenge, which he attributed to the Danes, in opposition to Inigo Jones, who thought the work Roman. Dryden's general praise of the new science, dating from Bacon, is interesting as reflecting something of the effect of his seven years' stay at Cambridge, from 1650 to 1657. Of the four men of science whom he praises, as successors of Bacon, all but Boyle are Cambridge men. Two of them, Harvey and Ent, were his own contemporaries, and Harvey's book on the circulation of the blood was actually

published at Cambridge during Dryden's under-
graduate days.

The introductory reference to Aristotle is
Dryden's first application of the couplet to
satire:—

> The longest tyranny that ever sway'd
> Was that wherein our ancestors betray'd
> Their free-born reason to the Stagirite,
> And made his torch their universal light.
> So truth, while only one supplied the state,
> Grew scarce and dear, and yet sophisticate;
> Until 'twas bought, like empiric wares or charms,
> Hard words seal'd up with Aristotle's arms.

In the following verses note the musical effect
produced by the repetition in three successive lines
of the same metrical pause—after the fourth syllable
—followed in each case by a similar clause. The
last two lines are a characteristic allusion to the
contemporary dream of the 'noble savage':—

> Columbus was the first that shook his throne,
> And found a temperate in a torrid zone,
> The feverish air ˅ fann'd by a cooling breeze,
> The fruitful vales ˅ set round with shady trees,
> And guiltless men, ˅ that danc'd away their time,
> Fresh as their groves and happy as their clime.

The musical effect may be partly unconscious; at
any rate there are some poor verses in the poem,
such, for instance, as the last of the lines in which,
again showing his interest in contemporary science,
he compares Charleton's cosmopolitan reputation
to the travels of light:—

Whose fame, not circumscrib'd with English ground,
Flies like the nimble journeys of the light,
And is, like that, unspent too in its flight.

Then we come to a much finer piece of work.
Lady Castlemaine, Barbara Palmer, afterwards
Duchess of Cleveland—her character is not material
in this connexion—had patronised and rescued
Dryden's first play *The Wild Gallant* at the time
of its unsuccessful production on the stage early
in 1663, and to her an Epistle was addressed in
gratitude by the poet. There is evidence that
Dryden himself claimed merit for this poem of his.
Thus a contemporary satirist (in the *Session of the
Poets*, published 1670) writes :—

> Dryden, who one would have thought had more wit,
> The censure of every man did disdain,
> Pleading some pitiful rhymes he had writ
> In praise of the Countess of Castlemaine.

Scott's explanation of this allusion is not satisfactory;
he seeks in the Epistle itself authority for Dryden's
'pleading,' and finds it in the lines :—

> True poets empty fame and praise despise ;
> Fame is the trumpet, but your smile the prize.

But this does not show that he 'pleaded' these lines
as a sufficient answer to universal censure; indeed
Lady Castlemaine's opinion on *The Wild Gallant*,
a prose work, could not prove its author's poetical
merit. What the lines in the *Session* show is that
Dryden himself approved what the satirist pleases
to call the 'pitiful rhymes' addressed to Lady
Castlemaine. The explanation of Dryden's high

opinion of this Epistle is perhaps that it is his first masterpiece, the first poem, that is to say, without technical flaw which he had produced. There is, for instance, no case of false emphasis upon the rhyme, such as occurs in the immediately preceding Epistle to Dr Charleton: 'Flies...and is unspent *in its flight.*' Moreover, the gay extravagance of the tone, its adaptation to its subject—it was the first time that he had addressed a lady—the swift movement of the verse, and the clearness of expression and thought mark it for distinction among Dryden's works. I quote the whole:—

As seamen, shipwrack'd on some happy shore,
Discover wealth in lands unknown before,
And what their art had labour'd long in vain
By their misfortunes happily obtain,
So my much-envied Muse, by storms long tost,
Is thrown upon your hospitable coast,
And finds more favour by her ill success
Than she could hope for by her happiness.
Once Cato's virtue did the gods oppose,
While they the victor, he the vanquish'd chose:
But you have done what Cato could not do,
To choose the vanquish'd and restore him too.
Let others still triumph and gain their cause
By their deserts or by the world's applause;
Let merit crowns, and justice laurels give,
But let me happy by your pity live.
True poets empty fame and praise despise;
Fame is the trumpet, but your smile the prize.
You sit above, and see vain men below
Contend for what you only can bestow;
But those great actions others do by chance,
Are, like your beauty your inheritance:

So great a soul, such sweetness joined in one,
Could only spring from noble Grandison.
You, like the stars, not by reflection bright,
Are born to your own heaven, and your own light;
Like them are good, but from a nobler cause,
From your own knowledge, not from Nature's laws.
Your power you never use but for defence,
To guard your own or others' innocence:
Your foes are such as they, not you, have made,
And virtue may repel, though not invade.
Such courage did the ancient heroes show,
Who, when they might prevent, would wait the blow;
With such assurance as they meant to say,
We will o'ercome, but scorn the safest way.
What farther fear of danger can there be?
Beauty, which captives all things, sets me free.
Posterity will judge by my success
I had the Grecian poet's happiness,
Who, waving plots, found out a better way;
Some god descended and preserv'd the play.
When first the triumphs of your sex were sung
By those old poets, Beauty was but young,
And few admir'd the native red and white,
Till poets dress'd them up to charm the sight;
So Beauty took on trust, and did engage
For sums of praises till she came to age.
But this long growing debt to poetry
You justly, Madam, have discharg'd to me,
When your applause and favour did infuse
New life to my condemn'd and dying Muse.

Scott is too severe on the comparison with
'Cato's virtue'; he writes: 'There is however
little propriety in comparing the influence of the
royal mistress to the virtue of Cato.' But it is to
be remembered that 'the gods,' opposed by Lady

Castlemaine, are only theatrical critics, and that 'Cato' is merely an equivalent for judgement independent of fortune. Lucan's line is a stock quotation and the familiarity with it of the reader is assumed. The 'ancient heroes,' who waited the blow that they might have forestalled, are the combatants in the deliberate battles of Homer's Trojans and Greeks. The 'Grecian poet' is Euripides, and the descending god is the *deus ex machina*. To discuss the importance to Euripidean drama of the introduction of the *deus ex machina* would carry us too far from our proper subject; those who are interested will find my opinions expressed in my writings on Euripides, in particular in *Euripides the Rationalist*. To suppose, as Dryden appears to do, that Euripides paid no attention to the plots of his plays is sheer nonsense.

Were all these allusions intelligible to Lady Castlemaine? Presumably they were. The admirable nonsense of the conclusion—wit and beauty both complimented—is certainly not adapted to a stupid person.

The metrical skill is far beyond anything we have yet seen; note for instance the effect of the three strong monosyllables at the end of the fifth line: 'by stórms lóng tóst.' But if we are to ask whether the poem is really flawless, we must answer No; there is at least one objectionable metrical effect in the tenth line: 'he the vanquĭsh'd chose.' '-quish'd' is an uncomfortable syllable to shorten, especially before such a sound as 'chose,' and

though this defect could be avoided by the trans-
position of the two clauses—'while he the vanquish'd,
they the victor chose'—we should still be left with
the Latinism in the use of *while*, which, like the
Latin *dum*, is here used in the sense 'inasmuch as,'
referring back to the word 'once': once, namely
when he chose the vanquished, Cato opposed the
gods. But it is not easy to find any other flaw in
the poem.

The next Epistle, addressed to Lee and prefixed
to his tragedy published in 1677, has no metrical
flaws and no conceits. It contains the often quoted
lines :—

> Prizes would be for lags of slowest pace,
> Were cripples made the judges of the race.

Lee had written complimentary lines to Dryden
on the production, shortly before, of *The State of
Innocence*, and Dryden's opening lines, as I have
said, show that he was aware that he laid himself
open to a charge of 'log-rolling' :—

> The blast of common censure could I fear,
> Before your play my name should not appear;
> For 'twill be thought, and with some colour too,
> I pay the bribe I first receiv'd from you;
>
>   *   *   *   *   *   *
>
> Such libels private men may well endure,
> When States and Kings themselves are not secure.

The suggestion that 'States' and 'Kings' may be
accused of mutual flattery is perhaps an allusion to
the political 'approach' to Holland, due to Danby's
policy and the marriage of the Princess Mary with

William of Orange, which took place in the year
1677.

The Epistle to the Earl of Roscomon was
prefixed in 1684 to an *Essay on Translated Verse*
by the Roscomon of Pope's *Epistles* who, among
the poets of the reign of Charles II, 'only boasts
unspotted bays.' Johnson in his *Life of Roscomon*
blames Dryden's praise as exaggerated, and it
certainly is excessive, but the poem is well worth
reading. It opens with a purely imaginary sketch
of the history of poetry : art transplanted from
Egypt or Phoenicia to Greece, there developed into
poetry and thence passed to Rome ; the interest to
the student of Dryden lies in his view of rhymed
verse :—

> Till barbarous nations and more barbarous times
> Debas'd the majesty of verse to rhymes ;
> Those rude at first ; a kind of hobbling prose,
> That limp'd along and tinkl'd in the close.

Then followed the Italian poetry of Dante and
Petrarch, in whom

> we see
> What rhyme improv'd in all its height can be ;
> At best a pleasing sound and fair barbarity.

He proceeds to praise aristocratic authors :—

> To what perfection will our tongue arrive,
> How will invention and translation thrive,
> When authors nobly born will bear their part,
> *   *   *   *   *   *
> How will sweet Ovid's ghost be pleas'd to hear
> His fame augmented by a British peer.

The reader is reminded of the well known bathos in Pope's address to Murray,

> Grac'd as thou art, with all the power of words,
> So known, so honour'd at the House of Lords.

Roscomon, who subsequently published commendatory verses on Dryden's *Religio Laici*, is sometimes lax in metre :—

> Let free impartial men from Dryden learn
> Mysterious secrets of high concern,

or if a proposed emendation of this last line, by the insertion of 'a' before 'high,' be accepted, see the later line :—

> Hath too much mercy to send them to hell.

One strange slip in the metre we may note in the second of the following lines from Dryden's own poem :—

> Now let the few belov'd by Jove, and they
> Whom *infus'd* Titan form'd of better clay,
> On equal terms with ancient wit engage,
> Nor mighty Homer fear, nor sacred Virgil's page.

The next few Epistles call for little comment. It is interesting to note, in the Epistle to Higden (written probably in 1686), Dryden's rebuke of personal satire. Higden had translated the *Tenth Satire* of Juvenal, and Dryden compliments him on his own approximation to the manner of Horace, rather than to that of the author whom he was translating :—

> Yet you, my friend, have temper'd him so well,
> You make him smile in spite of all his zeal:

An art peculiar to yourself alone,
To join the virtues of two styles in one.

and speaking of personal satire, Dryden continues :—

It costs our quiet and content of mind,
And when 'tis compass'd leaves a sting behind.
Suppose I had the better end of the staff,
Why should I help the ill-natur'd world to laugh?
'Tis all alike to them who gets the day ;
They love the spite and mischief of the fray.
No, I have cur'd myself of that disease,
Nor will I be provok'd but when I please.

The Epistle to Etherege, written between 1685 and 1688, is a reply to one from Etherege to Lord Middleton. It does not deserve Scott's praise: 'Dryden happily retorts upon the witty knight with his own weapons...and acquits himself as well in the light arms of a polite and fashionable courtier, as when he wields the trenchant brand of his own keen satire.' The Epistle is written in octosyllabic verse, a metre which, as we know from the *Essay on Satire*, Dryden despised. The poems of both Etherege and Dryden are quite unquotable ; but in Dryden's lines we may note the contemptuous allusion to Buckingham's *Rehearsal* :—

The Duke St Aignon made a play.
If Gallic wit convince you scarce,
His Grace of Bucks has made a farce ;
And you, whose comic wit is terse all,
Can hardly fall below Rehearsal.
Then finish what you have began,
But scribble faster if you can :
For yet no George, to our discerning,
Has writ without a ten years' warning.

The Address to Sir Godfrey Kneller, written at some undetermined date before 1694, is not very interesting. In it, as in the Epistle to Roscomon, we find Dryden's view of the effect of rhyme upon poetry :—

> Then all the Muses in one ruin lie,
> And rhyme began to enervate poetry.

and in the next line he condemns 'a stupid military state,' thus recalling to our notice the marked absence in his lines on Oliver Cromwell of any commendation of military despotism. Later we have one of his frequent allusions to Eden, and learn that the art of poetry is older than the art of painting :—

> Our arts are sisters, though not twins in birth,
> For hymns were sung in Eden's happy earth
> By the first pair, while Eve was yet a saint,
> Before she fell with pride and learn'd to paint.
> Forgive the allusion; 'twas not meant to bite,
> But Satire will have room, where'er I write.

Since the days of Eden, however, painting has made the better bargain with the times :—

> Thy pencil speaks the tongue of every land.

But in neither art is there any room for big work : Kneller produces portraits; Dryden has no opportunity for the epic which was his ambition. Then follows a satire on mankind's desire for portraiture :—

> Good Heaven! that sots and knaves should be so vain,
> To wish their vile resemblance may remain,
> And stand recorded at their own request,
> To future days, a libel or a jest!

Time will not permit me to quote the fine lines in the Epistle to Congreve (1693 or 1694) beginning 'O that your brows my laurel had sustained' (this same laurel a few years later, 1698, he proposes to resign to Granville); but the Epistle to Congreve must not be overlooked by a student of Dryden.

The Epistle to Motteux, a Huguenot who fled to this country after the Revocation of the Edict of Nantes, and became a successful playwright, was published in 1698 and is mainly interesting for its allusion to Jeremy Collier's attack on the immorality and profaneness of the English stage, which had appeared a few months earlier. Dryden's dislike of clerics[1], and his explanation of this sentiment, comes out in the following lines :—

> What I have loosely or profanely writ
> Let them to fires, their due desert, commit:
> Nor, when accus'd by me, let them complain;
> Their faults, and not their function, I arraign.
> Rebellion, worse than witchcraft, they pursued;
> The pulpit preach'd the crime, the people rued.
> The stage was silenc'd; for the saints would see
> In fields perform'd their plotted tragedy.
> But let us first reform, and then so live
> That we may teach our teachers to forgive;
> Our desk be plac'd below their lofty chairs;
> Ours be the practice, as the precept theirs.

The Address to Motteux concludes in a strain of extravagant adulation, which can hardly be sincere :—

[1] See also below, p. 148.

But whence art thou inspir'd, and thou alone,
To flourish in an idiom not thy own?

*   *   *   *   *   *

Words, once my stock, are wanting to commend
So great a poet and so good a friend.

The Epistle to his cousin, John Driden of Chesterton, was written in the last year of Dryden's life and published shortly before his death in 1700. John Driden was a squire living at Chesterton, near Stilton in Huntingdonshire, a member of Parliament, belonging to the 'Country Party' whose politics were in opposition to the government of William III, and a bachelor. On the latter point, as has been seen, he is congratulated by Dryden :—

Minds are so hardly match'd that even the first,
Though pair'd by Heaven, in Paradise were curs'd.

and recurring to the problem of the Temptation, a favourite subject with him, he concludes :—

Each might have stood perhaps, but each alone ;
Two wrestlers help to pull each other down.

In his picture of the hare as an emblem of human life, we have an autobiographical touch ; during his later years, Dryden constantly visited his native county of Northampton :—

The hare in pastures or in plains is found,
Emblem of human life ; who runs the round,
And, after all his wandering ways are done,
His circle fills and ends where he begun,
Just as the setting meets the rising sun.

That the allusion in the above lines is a personal

one is to my mind proved by the immediately
following allusions to James II, then living in exile
at St Germain :—

> Thus princes ease their cares; but happier he,
> Who seeks not pleasure through necessity,
> Than such as once on slippery thrones were plac'd,
> And chasing, sigh to think themselves are chas'd.

The last word is a Gallicism almost amounting to
a pun, for 'chased' there means of course *chassé*,
'driven away,' not 'hunted,' while the earlier
'chasing' alludes to the hunting in the famous
forest of St Germain.

In the next lines where the art of the physician
is depreciated, and scientific curiosity discouraged,
the opportunity is seized for an attack upon Sir
Richard Blackmore, the poet and physician of the
day, who had published a translation of Virgil :—

> But Maurus sweeps whole parishes, and peoples every grave,
> And no more mercy to mankind will use
> Than when he robb'd and murder'd Maro's muse.

But some use there is in drugs, and with the
problem of the Temptation still haunting him, he
writes of quinine or Peruvian bark as it was then
called :—

> The tree of knowledge, once in Eden plac'd,
> Was easy found, but was forbid the taste ;
> O, had our grandsire walk'd without his wife,
> He first had sought the better plant of life !
> Now both are lost : yet wandering in the dark,
> Physicians for the tree have found the bark.

The politics of John Driden, and his position
as a member of Parliament, give Dryden the

opportunity of describing the conduct of those who, using the just mean,

> Nor gratify whate'er the great desire,
> Nor grudging give what public needs require.

where note the Latinisms 'gratify whate'er' and 'nor grudging give,' in the sense 'and give without grudging.' His own policy is expressed a few lines later :—

> Safe in ourselves, while on ourselves we stand,
> The sea is ours, and that defends the land.

Some reflexions on Dutch valour here followed, but were omitted in the published poem at the request of John Driden, and we pass on to a description of Prerogative and Privilege as two balanced streams:—

> One must not ebb nor t'other overflow.
>   *   *   *   *   *
> When both are full,—

they are like—what ?—the rivers that watered the garden of Eden ! The garden of Eden again for the third time in this poem !

> When both are full, they feed our blest abode,
> Like those that water'd once the Paradise of God.

After a complimentary reference to the patriots who resisted Charles I—a passage reflecting Dryden's real feeling[1], though invidiously meant as a side-stroke against the support of William III by the City :—

> Such was your generous grandsire, free to grant
> In parliaments that weigh'd their Prince's want:

[1] See above, pp. 19, 20.

But so tenacious of the common cause
As not to lend the king against his laws;

the poem concludes with a characteristic instance of Dryden's recklessness in facile compliment to the person or, it may be, the assembly that he is addressing: with apology, he equals his cousin to himself:—

Nor think the kindred Muses thy disgrace;
A poet is not born in every race.
Two of a house few ages can afford,
One to perform, another to record.
Praiseworthy actions are by thee embrac'd;
And 'tis my praise to make thy praises last.
For even when death dissolves our human frame,
The soul returns to Heaven from whence it came,
Earth keeps the body, verse preserves the fame.

III

ABSALOM AND ACHITOPHEL

THE fourteen years between the appearance of
Annus Mirabilis and *Absalom and Achitophel* were
mainly occupied by Dryden with dramatic work.
As drama, the work was unsatisfactory; Dryden
himself, it is true, makes a case for his successive
attempts, but tells us that one play only—*All for
Love,* on the subject of Shakespeare's *Antony and
Cleopatra* and written in blank verse—was written
'for himself[1].' His comedies, in prose, were not on
the whole successful; his tragedies or heroic plays,
on the other hand, were very popular and had made
him famous by the year 1671 when an attack was made
upon him in Buckingham's play of *The Rehearsal,*
under the name of 'Bayes,' an allusion to his recent
laureateship. The tragedies were almost wholly in
rhyme—ten-syllabled couplets of course—neither
the large stanza nor the so-called 'Pindaric' form of
verse, with its irregular rhymes, being conceivable
as the common material for drama.

The heroic play falls outside the scheme of these
lectures; here I can only briefly note that Dryden

[1] See below, p. 238.

was without dramatic faculty proper—the power, that is, to conceive character and express it in dialogue—nor was he skilful in the invention of a story. Thus he necessarily relied on the quality of his verse, its smartness, point, and music, qualities, in fact, such as are shown in his Address to Lady Castlemaine. Rapid production was necessary for profit, and this necessity gave him immense practice in the making of the heroic couplet. What he said at the end of his life about his facility for producing verse, by which he meant the couplet, was probably true by the year 1680 :—

> Thoughts, such as they are, come crowding in so fast upon me, that my only difficulty is to choose or to reject, to run them into verse, or to give them the other harmony of prose : I have so long studied and practised both, that they are grown into a habit, and become familiar to me. (*Preface to the Fables*, 1700.)

But hitherto he had made no worthy application of this skill. Had Dryden died in 1680, when he was approaching the age of 50 years, he would hardly have left with posterity a second-rate reputation : *Annus Mirabilis* was not sufficient in finish, and the *Epistles* were not substantial enough.

His ambition is shown in *Annus Mirabilis* and definitely explained in the Preface to that poem. He wanted a story combining reality with greatness of national and public interest, to be treated with a corresponding elevation of style after the accepted method of the classical epic. But in *Annus Mira-bilis* he attained only a limited success : history would not present a theme of convenient unity and classical ornament was ill adapted to familiar detail.

His opportunity came with the crisis of 1678–1681, and the proposal to exclude from the succession to the throne the King's brother, the Duke of York, in favour of his illegitimate son, the Duke of Monmouth. Here was a national episode immensely important and exciting, with a compact, simple issue almost expressible as a single *situation*; the details and progress of the story might be omitted or summarised, and the characters merely described in epigrams, Dryden's forte, and not developed by self-expression, a thing that was beyond his powers.

Some knowledge of the politics of the moment, as seen from Dryden's point of view, is necessary to a comprehension of the poem; the following summary must here suffice. Dryden believed in the vital importance of the monarchy, as the basis of natural structure and the centre of sentiment. Recent events had provided an apparently decisive experiment on this point. The King had been opposed and dethroned with most plausible reason;—and here I would emphasise the point that we have no ground whatever to suppose that Dryden ever retracted the view of the contest between Charles I and the Parliament in which he was brought up. The execution of the King was another matter; but, as I have said before[1], Dryden never took the High Anglican, the 'Royal Martyr,' view. But in spite of the plausible reason, the result of the dethronement

[1] See above, p. 20.

of Charles I was the general collapse of the system of government, for it proved irreplaceable, except by military despotism or anarchy, from which a narrow escape was won by the restoration of the royal line.

Hereditary title then was apparently essential to the maintenance of monarchy, for a Parliamentary title was insecure and invited meddling; and the hereditary title did in fact—and this is a vital point—satisfy public sentiment. The earlier history of the country supplied decisive experiments. The Lancastrians, for instance, had a Parliamentary title to the throne, but the Wars of the Roses showed the weakness of their position; and an hereditary title was the foundation of the stability of the Tudors, for an essential condition of the accession of Henry VII was his marriage with Elizabeth, heiress to the title of Edward IV and the house of York. Later again the prevalence of a natural hereditary title over all legal arrangements was illustrated in the case of the family of Henry VII. After the succession, in due hereditary order, of Henry VIII's three children, Edward, Mary and Elizabeth, in spite of the will of Henry VIII, made after Parliamentary sanction, the succession passed without any difficulty to the natural heir, James VI of Scotland. In view therefore of past experience, attachment to hereditary succession was not necessarily a mere superstition.

But the circumstances of the royal family in 1678 put sentiment to a violent strain. There was

strong objection to a Roman Catholic Government
in England irrespective of questions of theology.
The alienation of the Church Lands presented
problems of great difficulty, as had been manifest
in the reign of Mary, and was again shown in the
formal renunciation by the English Benedictine
monks of the abbey-lands held by the Order before
the Reformation—a refusal of 'your gold' by 'that
pious Joseph in the Church' which however failed in
its purpose[1]. Further, the position of the English
Church was closely connected with the influence
of the Crown as 'Head of the Church,' and besides these general objections to a Roman Catholic
Government in England, there were special objections to the French Catholicism of the day, whose
unique pretension and intolerance had made of it an
instrument of despotic government, which passing
from measures of gradually increasing severity
against Protestants to the *dragonnades* of 1681, was
shortly to culminate in the Revocation, in 1685, of
the Edict of Nantes. The King was suspected,
and justly suspected, of French Catholicism, though
his disclaimer was generally believed by good subjects of the Crown; the heir to the throne, James,
Duke of York, was known to be a French Catholic,
and a man of obstinate and violent character. On
the other hand, James's eldest daughter, the heiress
to the throne in default of male issue, was a Protestant and was married to a Protestant prince.

---

[1] To this renunciation Dryden refers in his marginal note on
the above-quoted passage in *The Hind and the Panther* Pt. II 646.

And besides these uncertainties for the future, various acts of mismanagement on the part of the Government, as well as a certain amount of ill luck, had produced a feeling of general discontent.

In May 1679, there was introduced into the House of Commons a Bill proposing to exclude the Duke of York from the succession to the Crown, on the ground of his religion; the 'Exclusion Bill' was the work of the Whig party, led by the Earl of Shaftesbury. The Abhorrers, afterwards called Tories, were opposed to any alteration of the natural succession. A strong case could be made out on both sides, and the feeling throughout the country was increased by certain exasperating circumstances.

Chief among these was the Popish Plot. Wholesale allegations of conspiracy and disloyalty were brought by Titus Oates, and other scoundrels of his type, against the Roman Catholics; the Queen herself was accused of a proposal to assassinate the King. There was beyond all question much lying and immense exaggeration, but probably a foundation for some of the charges; in Dryden's words :—

> Succeeding times *will* equal folly call
> Believing nothing or believing all.

The Popish Plot temporarily strengthened the Exclusionist party, but ultimately discredited them, when the first panic was followed by a natural revulsion and disgust; it is this latter phase which is represented by Dryden's poem.

The other circumstance which increased the national tension was the claim of Monmouth, the King's eldest son. The Duke of Monmouth was notoriously illegitimate and his mother was a woman of no position, but he was a favourite of his father, and himself a striking figure. He was handsome, wealthy, gracious, and popular, and his popularity was increased by a vague and unfounded claim to legitimacy based on the reported marriage of Charles to his mother. By a fatal blunder or necessity on the part of the Exclusionist leaders, the Whig party favoured Monmouth's claim and threatened to force him on the King as his successor by a Parliamentary title. The policy was impossible; it roused a revolt of natural honesty, for there was no shred of evidence of Monmouth's legitimacy. The weakness of his title was pleaded by the Exclusionists as an advantage, on the ground that 'the weaker the title, the better the king.' But such an argument pointed directly to a republic and to anarchy, to the certainty of civil war such as had been recently experienced, and to the probability of invasion; for Mary, the legitimate Protestant heiress, was married to the Protestant prince who was next in succession after the family of James, Duke of York.

Nevertheless the Exclusion Bill was carried in the House of Commons. It was rejected in the House of Lords, largely owing to the exertions of Halifax, and the King thereupon dissolved Parliament. That the next Parliament was announced to meet at Oxford shows the exasperation of the situation; the City of London was the stronghold of the Whig party. This Oxford Parliament was almost immediately dissolved. The King was in an impregnable position; he need not summon Parliament for three years, for he did not want money and so could give time for sentiment and reason to prevail. By the end of 1681 the tide had turned, and till the tension was removed both the Duke of York and Monmouth were sent out of the country.

The actual motives and character of Shaftesbury we need not here discuss; in the royalist view he was the seducer of the young Monmouth. In July 1681 he was arrested on a charge of high treason and in November he was brought to trial in the City. By the favour of a London jury, who threw out the Bill, he escaped for the moment, but later he lost control of the City and the next year had to save his life by flying to Holland. Just before the first accusation came on for trial, in November 1681, Dryden brought out *Absalom and Achitophel*.

The poem is an announcement and a prophecy of the royal triumph, and an appeal to the nation for grateful acquiescence.

Its plan is one of extreme simplicity, a situation rather than a story. A young illegitimate prince is seduced into rebellion by the art of a treacherous statesman; he is taught to cultivate popularity and does so with dangerous success. All this is stated in outline and abstraction only. The prince's position becomes a national danger owing to the caprice of the mob. Sketches, again abstract with slight identifying touches, are given of his principal supporters and of some of the loyal minority. The King is moved to interfere. His protest and his paternal threat allay the tumult.

The tone in the main is lofty and dignified, especially in the principal parts, as for instance in the scene of the temptation and of the King's pronouncement. The speeches are proper to epic or grave drama, such as we should expect in a heroic poem or play; the work, indeed, is called by Dryden a poem and not a satire. Occasional archaisms, foreign to Dryden's own natural style, point directly to the influence of the English 'epics,' *The Faerie Queene* and *Paradise Lost*—this last then just coming, with Dryden's help, into fame and vogue. Take for instance, the line :—

Him staggering so when Hell's dire agent found...(373)

Such inversion is not common in Dryden, nor is it in the manner proper to a narrative about contemporary politicians, or historical personages as such ; it is obviously Miltonic, and a Latinism, and so carries with it a suggestion of Milton's Satan. And a comparison between the temptation of Monmouth and that of Adam is actually made by Dryden in the prefatory address, ' To the Reader ' :—

> But since the most excellent natures are always the most easy and, as being such, are the soonest perverted by ill counsels, especially when baited with fame and glory, it is no more a wonder that he withstood not the temptations of Achitophel than it was for Adam not to have resisted the two devils, the serpent and the woman.

Further, the verse, especially in these main parts of the structure, is the very purest in style and most musical in sound which Dryden could compass, that is to say, the best in its kind of which English has been found capable. And note that Dryden himself emphatically asks attention to this point. It is by sweetness of verse that the poem, otherwise perilous in theme, and to some repellent, is to win its way :—

> Yet if a poem have a genius, it will force its own reception in the world; for there is a sweetness in good verse, which tickles even while it hurts; and no man can be heartily angry with him who pleases him against his will.

There is however a difficulty in applying 'heroic' treatment to contemporary politics, owing to the familiarity of the subject-matter and of the terms. Hence there is a danger that the style would be degraded by these, not they elevated by the style, and the result be a clumsy mock-heroic not so intended by the writer. Even the words 'Parliament,' 'Chancellor,' 'Cabinet,' are dangerous ; much more 'Mayor,' 'Sheriff,' 'Jury'; and more still 'writ,' 'bill,' 'committee,' 'supply.'

This difficulty is met by the happy device of a Biblical parallel, where David, Absalom, and Achitophel represent respectively Charles, Monmouth, and Shaftesbury. Neither the Biblical parallel in general, nor even this particular parallel, was invented by Dryden. It was obvious enough, and it was indeed a common habit in political sermons to compare Charles with David. Indeed he had

been likened to David by Dryden himself in his
Astraea Redux (published in 1660) :—

> Thus banish'd David spent abroad his time,
> When to be God's anointed was his crime.

and Dryden had been pressed to develop the parallel
by Lee in the Commendatory Verses prefixed to the
State of Innocence seven years before :—

> Monarch of verse ! new themes employ thy pen.
> The troubles of majestic Charles set down ;
> Not David vanquish'd more to reach a crown.
> Praise him as Cowley did that Hebrew king :
> Thy theme's as great ; do thou as greatly sing.

The comparison between Absalom and Monmouth
had already been used by more than one writer in
prose and verse ; thus Scott quotes from a small
tract called *Absalom's Conspiracy: or the Tragedy
of Treason*, and this is not the only case. The
name of Absalom for Monmouth, like that of David
for the King, was probably common in sermons, and
the allusion could not be missed.

But Dryden was nevertheless profoundly original.
The Biblical parallel is used *to admit the ' heroic
style.'* ' Sanhedrin ' and 'Abbethdin' would bear a
treatment which ' Parliament ' and ' Chancellor '
could not, and in the same way generally the Biblical
terminology was a thing of dignity. It should be
noted that the actual parallel is very slight : there
is no ' Sanhedrin ' in the story of David, nor any
resemblance between the 'Sanhedrin' and the British
Parliament. Nor is there any attempt to press the
parallel ; the treatment of contemporary events on

abstract lines, and the comparison with the Biblical story, is necessary on pain of absurdity. The scheme is admirably conceived and carried out.

Even so the translation of modern terms into Biblical language might easily tire the reader and become silly. It does become so in the so-called *Second Part of Absalom and Achitophel,* a supplementary work in which Dryden had but a small share. There the characters are multiplied so as to suggest a whole House of Lords with Hebrew names, and to take a specific instance, Christopher Monck, second Duke of Albemarle, having become Chancellor of the University of Cambridge, is said to preside over 'the Prophets' school,' 'Prophets' being the term regularly applied to the clergy. Even Dryden's own contributions to Part II are open to the same objection. When he replies to the satirising poets, there is very little fun in using the names of 'Og' for Shadwell and 'Doeg' for Settle. To estimate *Absalom and Achitophel* fairly, and to feel it, Part I must be taken for what it is, a finished work, rounded, complete.

An important question to be determined is, in what sense is *Absalom and Achitophel* a 'satire'? It is not so described by the author, whose title for it is 'Absalom and Achitophel. A Poem'; and it should be compared, or rather contrasted, with his attack on Shaftesbury and his party in the following year, which he calls 'The Medal. A Satire against Sedition.' *Absalom and Achitophel* is however commonly classified as a satire. It does not fit any

other known class, such for instance as 'epic,' and
it does contain important satiric elements in the
portraits, of which the representation of Buckingham
as Zimri may be taken as a specimen. [The figure
of Achitophel is partly 'satiric,' that is to say, it is
intended as a hostile picture of the man Shaftesbury.]
And it is these elements or passages in the work,
partly because they are detachable and quotable,
that are perhaps the best known. But they do not
cover the type, and if we must classify the poem, it
is best to call it an '*epyllion*, or epic in miniature,
comprising satiric elements.' I emphasise the first
part of this description; the gorgeous Muse of
Satire comes sweeping by, draped in robes bor-
rowed from her more august sisters Epic and
Tragedy, but the robes are essential to the performance.

The work is really *unique*; there is no parallel
in Dryden or elsewhere known to me. It bears
no resemblance as a whole to Roman satire, as we
know it in Horace, Persius, and Juvenal. An analogy has been alleged to Juvenal's *Fourth Satire*.
That satire, it is true, is a story and does comprise
satiric portraits of individuals: Domitian summons
his council to discuss the cooking of a remarkably
fine turbot and the various councillors are described.
But it is more than doubtful if Dryden owed anything to this work. The formal resemblance is
slight, and the substance and spirit are totally different. Juvenal's piece is essentially dependent on
an undignified theme, Dryden's on a dignified one;

Juvenal neither gives nor could give anything like
the scene of the Temptation.

Still less does *Absalom and Achitophel* resemble
Dryden's own recipe or instructions for modern
satire, given in his *Discourse concerning the Original
and Progress of Satire*, a rambling and colloquial
essay, prefixed to translations from the Latin satirists
eleven years later, in 1693. There are reasons for
pressing this point. Dryden's incidental reference
to *Absalom and Achitophel* in his *Discourse* is loose
and injurious. He depreciates satire (by which he
means railing against individuals) as doubtfully legitimate, and this he does partly from religious motives,
malice and even revenge being unlawful. In this
attitude he is probably sincere; his own satires,
properly so-called, are almost all replies to attacks
made upon him. But he has a deeper reason for
his depreciation; 'satire' could hardly be sweet and
noble, and for these qualities, sweetness and nobility,
Dryden has a passion. This comes out in his comparison of Juvenal and Horace. Juvenal, he says
in the *Discourse*, is eloquent, indignant, violent;
Horace is playful, light, insinuating. Dryden personally prefers Juvenal for 'pleasure,' because his
tone admits a more 'sonorous and more noble' style,
and a more 'numerous'—by which he means musical
—verse, whereas Horace naturally adopts a conver-
sational tone and a style which Dryden calls 'low.'
Whether this is a just view we do not now enquire.
But in spite of his personal preference, Dryden
admits and insists that the playful, gentle tone of

Horace is in itself better and more conducive to the true end of satire : ' Let the chastisement of Juvenal be never so necessary...let him declaim as wittily and sharply as he pleases ; yet still the nicest and most delicate touches of satire consist in fine raillery.' In this connexion he cites his own Zimri (Buckingham), saying truly that he rather plays with Buckingham than denounces him, treating of his foibles ('blindsides'), and not, for instance, of his political perfidies and cruel vengeances: 'I avoided the mention of great crimes, and applied myself to the representing of blindsides and little extravagancies.' He has just stated that the character of Zimri is, in his opinion, 'worth the whole poem : it is not bloody, but it is ridiculous enough.' If by this statement Dryden means that the whole poem would be sufficiently justified by producing the passage on the character of Zimri, it may be true, but it is not important. If it means that, as a fact, the essential merit of *Absalom and Achitophel* lies in such passages, then it is an instance of Dryden's carelessness and habit of emphasising the theme of the moment. He did not seriously think so in 1693, or when he wrote *Absalom and Achitophel*, or ever.

It is a significant fact that in the *Discourse*, while professing to treat satire, Dryden is haunted and obsessed by 'epic' and 'heroic poetry.' He cannot get to his proper subject; a large part (about a fifth) of the essay is spent on Spenser, on Milton, on their machinery, on his own conceptions of better machinery, on the subjects on which he would himself like to write an epic, such as King Arthur and the Black Prince, on 'Guardian Angels of countries,' —all this most interestingly put but formally irrelevant. Dryden notes his own irrelevance and appears puzzled at it. It is not, however. so strange ; his own chief 'Satire' is really an epic, and is his nearest approach to his real ambition : 'an Heroic Poem is certainly the greatest work of human nature.'

The 'satire' in *Absalom and Achitophel* is toned down to suit his general purpose and to allow attractive sweetness. He says so in his Preface to the poem : ' I confess I have laid in for those [the more moderate sort], by rebating the satire, where justice would allow it, from carrying too sharp an edge,' where the reader should observe that the 'satire' which he rebates is not the poem as a whole, but the severity of personal passages. The character of Absalom is not a satire at all. For this there was no doubt a special motive in the King's affection for Monmouth : 'the fault on the right hand is to extenuate, palliate, and indulge; and, to confess freely, I have endeavoured to commit it. Besides the respect which I owe his birth, I have a greater for his heroic virtues ; and David himself could not be more tender of the young man's life, than I would be of his reputation.' In Achitophel the satire is much blunted and the traits generalised; in these respects it offers a strong contrast with the treatment in *The Medal.* Shaftesbury's physical infirmity and puny appearance is noted in our poem with a gentle touch :—

> A fiery soul, which working out its way,
> Fretted the pigmy body to decay
> And o'er-inform'd the tenement of clay.

This attitude was strengthened on a revision of the poem, and Shaftesbury is praised as a judge :—

> Yet fame deserv'd no enemy can grudge;
> The statesman we abhor, but praise the judge.
> In Israel's courts ne'er sat an Abbethdin
> With more discerning eyes or hands more clean,
> Unbrib'd, unsought, the wretched to redress,
> Swift of despatch, and easy of access.

Even the description of Oates (Corah) shows reserve. All this is congenial to Dryden's temper and necessary for the nobility and 'sweetness' of what, following his title, we must call the *poem*, which we may now consider in some detail.

The Poem

The central and all important episode is the Temptation. Here we must read minutely and with careful attention to metrical effects, in order to note the appeal of the actual verse.

Observe first the dignity of the introductory passage, and the rise in poetical ornament :—

> Achitophel still wants a chief, and none
> Was found so fit as warlike Absalon.
> Not that he wish'd his greatness to create,
> For politicians neither love nor hate;
> But, for he knew his title not allow'd
> Would keep him still depending on the crowd,
> That kingly power, thus ebbing out, might be
> Drawn to the dregs of a democracy.

Him he attempts with studied arts to please
And sheds his venom in such words as these.

(220 ff.)

The passage has two figures : 'ebbing out...
drawn to the dregs of a democracy' and 'sheds his
venom'; the first is a favourite figure of Dryden's
and is verbally repeated by him elsewhere (*Hind and
Panther* I 211); the other suggests both the serpent
and the toad of Milton (*P. L.* Books IX and IV)
whose style is also recalled by the Latin archaism
'him he attempts.'

The language of this passage is simplicity and
plainness itself; all the words are in current use.
Hence the effect of sneers produced by the two
words of Greek derivation, 'politicians' and 'democracy.' I do not mean that the effect of introducing
words of Greek derivation into a passage otherwise
purely English is necessarily sneering, but that it
marks some distinction. All good English com-
posers study this matter of 'keys' and utilise the
different sources of our language ; the point is vital.

Note also how, in the terse expression of policy
attributed to Shaftesbury, and its danger :—

But, for he knew his title not allow'd
Would keep him still depending on the crowd,
That kingly power, thus ebbing out, might be
Drawn to the dregs of a democracy.

absolutely no force is put upon the language to
adapt it to the verse-form.

So far for the introduction to Achitophel's speech.
The problem now before Dryden was, how to go up

from this level without rupture and to present the temptation as beautiful. He solves his problem thus :—

Auspicious prince, at whose nativity
Some royal planet rul'd the southern sky,
Thy longing country's darling and desire,
Their cloudy pillar and their guardian fire,
Their second Moses, whose extended wand
Divides the seas and shows the promis'd land,
Whose dawning day in every distant age
Has exercis'd the sacred prophet's rage,
The people's prayer, the glad diviner's theme,
The young men's vision, and the old men's dream,
Thee Saviour, thee the nation's vows confess,
And never satisfied with seeing bless :   241
Swift unbespoken pomps thy steps proclaim,
And stammering babes are taught to lisp thy name.
How long wilt thou the general joy detain,   244
Starve and defraud the people of thy reign?
Content ingloriously to pass thy days,
Like one of virtue's fools that feeds on praise ;
Till thy fresh glories, which now shine so bright,   248
Grow stale and tarnish with our daily sight.
Believe me, royal youth, thy fruit must be
Or gather'd ripe, or rot upon the tree.
Heaven has to all allotted, soon or late,
Some lucky revolution of their fate :
Whose motions if we watch and guide with skill,
(For human good depends on human will,)
Our fortune rolls as from a smooth descent
And from the first impression takes the bent ;
But, if unseiz'd, she glides away like wind
And leaves repenting folly far behind.
Now, now she meets you with a glorious prize
And spreads her locks before her as she flies.

Had thus old David, from whose loins you spring,
Not dar'd, when fortune call'd him to be King,
At Gath an exile he might still remain,   264
And Heaven's anointing oil had been in vain.
Let his successful youth your hopes engage,
But shun the example of declining age.
Behold him setting in his western skies,
The shadows lengthening as the vapours rise;
He is not now, as when, on Jordan's sand,   270
The joyful people throng'd to see him land,
Covering the beach and blackening all the strand,
But like the Prince of Angels, from his height
Comes tumbling downward with diminish'd light:
Betray'd by one poor plot to public scorn,
(Our only blessing since his curst return,)
Those heaps of people, which one sheaf did bind,
Blown off and scatter'd by a puff of wind.
What strength can he to your designs oppose,
Naked of friends, and round beset with foes?
If Pharaoh's doubtful succour he should use,   281
A foreign aid would more incense the Jews;
Proud Egypt would dissembled friendship bring,
Foment the war, but not support the King;
Nor would the royal party e'er unite
With Pharaoh's arms to assist the Jebusite;
Or, if they should, their interest soon would break
And with such odious aid make David weak.
All sorts of men, by my successful arts
Abhorring kings, estrange their alter'd hearts
From David's rule: and 'tis the general cry,   291
Religion, commonwealth, and liberty.
If you, as champion of the public good,
Add to their arms a chief of royal blood,   294
What may not Israel hope, and what applause
Might such a general gain by such a cause?
Not barren praise alone, that gaudy flower
Fair only to the sight, but solid power;

> And nobler is a limited command, 299
> Given by the love of all your native land,
> Than a successive title, long and dark,
> Drawn from the mouldy rolls of Noah's ark.

Endless observations might be made upon the passage; a few only can be here selected, thus :—

(1) A metrical analysis of the opening lines (230–243), the Invocation to Absalom, shows a persistence of verses divisible by their sense and their swing into two parts. Of this form there are two types represented respectively by the first and second lines. In the first line the break comes after the fourth syllable :—

> Auspicious prince, ˅ at whose nativity,

and in the second line after the fifth :—

> Some royal planet ˅ rul'd the southern sky.

The first eleven verses represent these two types in the following order : 1 of the first, 4 of the second, 4 of the first, 1 of the second, 1 of the first ; and the effect is to produce a certain spell on the ear. Then there is a sudden dissolution of this tension or spell in the next line (241), where the verse, though divisible, is unbalanced ; for the division, determined by the sense, occurs immediately before the last syllable :—

> And never satisfied with seeing ˅ bless :

Then, in the next line, a new division, after the sixth syllable, is introduced, the effect of which is to lay emphasis on the splendid phrase in the opening half :—

> Swift unbespoken pomps ˅ thy steps proclaim.

The allusion here is to the popular demonstrations which had accompanied Monmouth's progresses through the country after his return from abroad in 1679. In 'unbespoken' there is a touch of satire; in 'pomps' Dryden goes back to the history of the Greek word πέμπειν, with its associations and meaning, not of pageantry but of procession. The splendour of the phrase 'unbespoken pomps' is relieved against the plainness of the word 'swift' and the interruption of the general metrical scheme by the unexpected rhythm of the preceding line.

(2) The first proposal of royalty comes in the next lines (244 f.), where the *necessary* pause after 'people,' to save the sense, brings a surprise to the ear and so emphasises the suggested royalty :—

> How long wilt thou the general joy detain,
> Starve and defraud the people ˅ of thy reign.

(3) In *v.* 248, we may note the suggestive emphasis due to the slight drag in the rhythm produced by the five weighted monosyllables in its latter half :—

> Till thy fresh glories, which now shine so bright....

(4) The reception of Charles at Dover in May 1660 is described in the triplet, 270 ff., a variation of the couplet rarely used in this poem¹. Some effect is here certainly both felt and meant; for

¹ In the 1031 lines, the triplet occurs eight times. In the 456 lines of *Religio Laici* there are six triplets, and in the 572 lines of the First Part of *The Hind and the Panther* there are thirty-four.

note also the unique rhythm in the last line due
to the two trisyllabic words 'covering,' 'blackening,'
and compare with this the effect of the single trisyllabic 'lengthening' in *v.* 269 :—

> The shadows *lengthening* as the vapours rise.

What is the effect intended in the triplet ? Is not
the picture meant to be disagreeable ?—

> *Covering* the beach and *blackening* all the strand.

What does it call up to us ? Beetles ? Achitophel
undoubtedly means to sneer at royalist sentiment
and there is an involuntary recoil of feeling on
the crowd, the populace, as such. This leads on
consistently to his palpable sneer in the word
'tumbling':—

> Comes tumbling downward with diminish'd light, (274)

where the undignified words vaguely suggest the
collapse of a sort of cockchafer-glow-worm.

It is interesting to contrast this allusion by
Achitophel with Dryden's own description of the
same scene in his *Astraea Redux*:—

> Methinks I see those crowds on Dover's strand,
> Who in their haste to welcome you to land
> Chok'd up the beach with their still growing store
> And made a wilder torrent on the shore :
> While, spurr'd with eager thoughts of past delight,
> Those who had seen you court a second sight,
> Preventing still your steps and making haste
> To meet you often wheresoe'er you past. (276 ff.)

(5) In line 291 we find the only instance in
this speech of overlapping from the couplet before.

'From David's rule' is a corrective parenthesis qualifying the abhorrence of kings which, though representing Achitophel's real feeling, is contrary to his proposed intention of making Monmouth king. The apparent candour of Achitophel's conclusion that 'abhorring kings' leads to the desire for a 'commonwealth,' is skilfully turned by the later suggestion that 'nobler is a limited command' than a doubtful title.

The concluding lines of the speech refer to the special circumstances of Monmouth, who had no legal title but yet a sort of heirship. 'The mouldy rolls of Noah's ark' remind us of the prodigious pedigrees of the seventeenth century, tracing progenitors back to Adam,—in Wales even beyond!— and the heraldic *sound* of the earlier line (294):—

> *Add* to their *arms* a *chief* of royal blood,

strengthens the implication of virtual legitimacy.

Some such detailed examination as this of Achitophel's great speech helps us to understand its effect on contemporary hearers. The vocabulary was one of the points that attracted immediate notice. Thus in the Recommendatory Verses prefixed to later editions of the poem, Dryden is described as a converted Milton :—

> As if a Milton from the dead arose,
> Fil'd off the rust, and the right party chose.

and complimented on his 'new speech,' that is, on the novelty of his language :—

> The dialect, as well as sense, invents,
> And, with his poem, a new speech presents.

I leave the consideration of metrical effects in the scene of the Temptation, and pass to other points deserving comment.

In *v.* 281 Pharaoh stands for Louis XIV and 'the Jebusites' for the Catholics. These Biblical characters have no real relation to the story of David, and the introduction of them illustrates Dryden's method throughout the poem. The inverse is also true : not all 'Charles' is 'David,' any more than all 'David' is 'Charles.' Allusions to actual history under a Biblical form need not and must not be interpreted too strictly ; sometimes the historical facts, at others the Biblical parallel is the more prominent in Dryden's mind. Several examples of this may be found. For instance, 'Amnon's murder' (39)—an allusion which 'has never been satisfactorily explained,' writes Prof. J. Churton Collins in his note on the passage—need not have any precise analogy in the known actions of Monmouth. Again the couplet :—

> And Corah might for Agag's murder call,
> In terms as coarse as Samuel used to Saul.

> (676 f.)

is referred by commentators, supported by the bookseller's 'Key' (under the heading *Agag*) in the posthumous edition of 1716, to the death of Sir Edmund Berry Godfrey, the magistrate who took the evidence at the beginning of the Popish Plot, and was shortly afterwards found dead under circumstances suggestive of murder. No satisfactory explanation of his death was offered, but the incident led to the accusation of the Catholics and gave impetus to the plot. Mr Churton Collins and others interpret these lines as meaning that Corah (Oates) instigated the murder of Godfrey. But this interpretation does not explain the words 'call for Agag's murder,' nor the 'coarse terms,' nor the allusion to Samuel and Saul (*I Sam.* xv). What I take Dryden to mean is that Oates had the impudence to abuse and threaten the King, when he showed an inclination to rescue some of the victims of Oates's perjuries. The context in Dryden's poem makes this clear : describing Corah (Oates), he writes :—

> His zeal to Heaven made him his Prince despise,
> And load his person with indignities.
> But zeal peculiar privilege affords,
> Indulging latitude to deeds and words :
> And Corah might for Agag's murder call,
> In terms as coarse as Samuel used to Saul.

No precise Biblical analogy is to be found—or sought ; Agag in fact was not 'murdered' at all. But Samuel as a prophet stands for a cleric (which Oates was), here as throughout the poem, and he overruled, in opprobrious terms, a king disposed to clemency ; this is enough for Dryden.

> For govern'd by the moon, the giddy Jews
> Tread the same track when she the prime renews :
> And once in twenty years their scribes record,
> By natural instinct they change their lord. (216 ff.)

Here the historical references are to the changes of government which took place within the memory of living men at intervals of about twenty years : the

Long Parliament met in 1640, Charles II was restored in 1660, and the crisis of the Exclusion Bill was in 1680. Dryden's jest is that everything recurs, 'treads the same track,' as does even the inconstant moon when 'she the prime renews.' This last reference is not, I think, to the monthly change of the moon, but to the recurrence of similarity in the relative position of sun and moon which takes place about every twenty years[1].

> A fiery soul, which working out its way,
> Fretted the pigmy body to decay
> And o'er-inform'd the tenement of clay.   (156 ff.)

In this description of Achitophel Dryden is thinking of the Aristotelian theory in which soul represents form and body represents matter. The word 'o'er-inform'd' is used in the Aristotelian sense, and the 'fiery soul' recalls the theories of certain Greek philosophers. The classical associations of the passage are reinforced by the word 'pigmy' which is

[1] The phrase 'renew the prime' occurs in the Third Part of *The Hind and the Panther* (536) where, as here, it plainly means 'recurs to the original starting point'; the statement in Christie's Glossary that prime = spring (with a reference to *The Hind and the Panther* III 536 only), does not apply to the passage in *Absalom and Achitophel*, and is in any case somewhat misleading as to the exact meaning of the phrase even in *The Hind and the Panther*.

When the discrepancy between sun and moon is reconciled by an adjustment of the Calendar, the moon may be said to recur to her original standing point, to 'renew the prime'; the cycle of the Jewish Calendar, at the end of which such a readjustment was made, was a period of 19 years.

Greek in origin. What Dryden intends to convey is that in Shaftesbury there was too much 'form' for the 'matter.'

> Some thought they God's anointed meant to slay
> By guns, invented since full many a day :   (130 f.)

These lines have been supposed to allude to Oates's accusation against certain Catholics (Pickering and Grove) of having pistols for the assassination of the King. But this does not explain Dryden's language. The couplet is a satiric extravagance : the accusers were ready for any *absurdity*, even to the point of accusing their victims of possessing weapons not yet invented. The next two lines make the point clear :—

> Our author swears it not; but who can know
> How far the Devil and Jebusites may go?   (132 f.)

> He to his brother gives supreme command,
> To you a legacy of barren land,
> Perhaps the old harp on which he thrums his lays
> Or some dull Hebrew ballad in your praise.
>
>   (437 ff.)

The points here are clearly not Biblical; David had no brother answering to the Duke of York. They are therefore presumably historical, but are vaguely touched. 'Supreme command' is applicable to James, Duke of York, who was governing Scotland, where he had been sent in 1679 to a sort of honourable banishment, as High Commissioner. 'Barren land' is applicable to the Scottish estates

of the Duchess of Monmouth, Anne Scott, Countess
of Buccleugh, the 'charming Annabel' of the poem
(34); for the 'barrenness' of Scotland is a persistent
English jest or sneer, as readers of Dr Johnson's
account of his travels there will remember. Are
then 'the harp' and the 'ballad' also pertinent?
Not necessarily; but they are probably sneers at
the position of a Scottish feudal prince, as a patron
of minstrels. The Buccleugh family were famous
for such patronage both then and later, as we are
reminded in Scott's *Lay of the Last Minstrel*, and
Anne Scott, Countess of Buccleugh, was herself
generous to all poets and Dryden's earliest and
best patron.

The question further arises whether in this
passage (440) 'Hebrew' is to be interpreted as
'Scottish.' It is not so taken in an earlier passage
(128):—

> Which Hebrew priests the more unkindly took,
> Because the fleece accompanies the flock,

where the 'Hebrew priests' are apparently merely
the normal English (that is to say, the Protestant)
clergy as opposed to the Jebusites, who always
stand for the Catholics. Hebrew, in fact, is not
distinguished from Jewish, the opposition being
between Jews and Jebusites. But in our present
passage, the 'Hebrew ballad' (440), neither 'English' nor 'Protestant' gives sense or point.

Now, there is an odd fact to remark in the use
of the name 'Hebron.' In the original poem, the

First Part of *Absalom and Achitophel*, the name occurs once :—

> Who banish'd David did from Hebron bring,
> And with a general shout proclaim'd him King. (59 f.)

Here 'Hebron' apparently stands for the Continent, perhaps in particular the Low Countries or Brussels, from which Charles was brought to England ; and this notwithstanding the later passage (264) where David is described as having been called to be king from Gath, Gath being taken very loosely from *I Sam.* xxvii 2 ff., where David as an exile is said to be residing in Gath.   There is thus no consistency in Dryden's use of the Biblical names, but it is clear that Hebron in Part I does not mean Scotland.

Why then is Hebron assumed to be Scotland in Part II of *Absalom and Achitophel* and in Tonson's ' Key '—this last however a mere compilation without Dryden's authority, reprinted by modern commentators.   In Part II (320), Judas, who stands for the plotter Ferguson, is called a 'false Hebronite ' ; in *v.* 328, the Scots are described as 'men of Hebron' ; and two lines lower Phaleg, who stands for Forbes, is called 'the lay Hebronite.'   So through the whole passage Hebron clearly represents Scotland, and this passage, it should be noted, is in the part of the poem which was mainly written by Dryden himself.   In other parts also of Part II, Hebron stands for Scotland, in particular as the place of the Duke of York's exile.   Thus :—

From Hebron now the suffering heir return'd.   (793)

As nobly has his sway in Hebron shown,
How fit to inherit godlike David's throne.   (803 f.)

Still Hebron's honour'd happy soil retains
Our royal hero's beauteous dear remains.   (1065 f.)

the meaning of these last two lines being that the
Duchess of York had been left in Scotland, whither
James was going back to fetch her!

Now if 'Hebrew' were read as meaning Scottish
in the passage under discussion in Part 1 (440), the
use of ' Hebron ' for Scotland in the Second Part
would be accounted for.   And Hebrew may easily
be there so read, the 'supreme command' being a
command in Scotland, and the 'barren land' being
estates in Scotland.   Hence if some place-name for
Scotland were wanted answering to the adjective
'Hebrew' for Scottish, the connexion of sound would
easily suggest ' Hebron.'

Even in the earlier passage in Part 1 where
'Hebrew priests' are mentioned (128), the reference
may be chiefly to the Presbyterian rather than to
the Anglican clergy, for the ministers of the Estab-
lishment were not dependent on the 'fleece of the
flock.'

O! had he been content to serve the crown
With virtues only proper to the gown,...
David for him his tuneful harp had strung
And Heaven had wanted one immortal song. (192 ff.)

The last two lines of this passage, which occurs in
the description of Achitophel, have given rise to
some extravagant interpretations.   It has even been

suggested that the 'immortal song' was Dryden's
own poem, which would not have been written had
Achitophel been 'content to serve the crown.' Clearly
the allusion here to Shaftesbury is very vague and
implies little more than that but for his intrigues on
the present occasion he would have retained the
King's approbation and an honourable place in
history.   The Biblical allusion on the other hand is
plain.   Dryden is referring to the Third Psalm:
Domine, quid multiplicati, 'Lord, how are they increased that trouble me,' which is described in the
Authorised Version as 'A Psalm of David when he
fled from Absalom his son,' and where in modern
annotated editions references are given to *II Sam.*
xv–xviii.   Had Absalom not been induced by Achitophel's counsels to rebel against David this Psalm
would not have been written, and the number of
those 'immortal songs' would have been less by one.
This is a case where the reference is inappropriate
to Charles and the contemporary events, and where
the Biblical parallel, the original David and Achitophel, is paramount in Dryden's thoughts.

But indeed, apart from Biblical parallels in the
poem, personal allusions should not be too much
sought. Take for instance the passage where Dryden,
speaking of Achitophel, writes :—

> And all to leave what with his toil he won
> To that unfeather'd two-legg'd thing, a son,
> Got, while his soul did huddled notions try,
> And born a shapeless lump, like anarchy.   (169 ff.)

The third Earl of Shaftesbury, Achitophel's

grandson, is said to have resented this description
of his father. If so he did not show much wit. The
second Earl was not deformed but on the contrary
a handsome man. This fact, however, is irrelevant.
All 'sons' are 'unfeathered two-legged things' and
'born shapeless.' Dryden's point is that wealth and
rank must pass to a thing so uncertain in quality as
a baby; the particular qualities of Lord Ashley are
irrelevant.

The epic dignity of the poem is highest in the
scene of the Temptation, in Absalom's appeal to
the people (698 ff.) and in the Conclusion (939 ff.).
The Conclusion is selected for special praise in one
of the four Recommendatory Verses prefixed under
Dryden's sanction to the later editions :—

> Scarce a diviner flame inspir'd the king,
> Of whom thy muse does so sublimely sing,
> Not David's self could in a nobler verse
> His gloriously offending son rehearse,
> Though in his breast the prophet's fury met
> The father's fondness, and the poet's wit.

Two passages only in the Conclusion can be referred
to here; first the magnificent lines of the King's
pronouncement :—

> Unsatiate as the barren womb or grave,
> God cannot grant so much as they can crave.
> What then is left but with a jealous eye
> To guard the small remains of royalty?
> The law shall still direct my peaceful sway,
> And the same law teach rebels to obey:
> Votes shall no more establish'd power control,
> Such votes as make a part exceed the whole.

No groundless clamours shall my friends remove
Nor crowds have power to punish ere they prove;
For gods and godlike kings their care express
Still to defend their servants in distress.   (987 ff.)

Note here the distinction given by the careful introduction of Latin associations in the first line and
again in the concluding couplet; the Latin word
'unsatiate' replaces the 'never satisfied' of *Prov.*
xxx 15 f., from which the comparison is taken, and
the uncolloquial but classical use of the word 'express' is a Latinism.

Later in the speech the King suggests that the
false witnesses will turn against the Whigs; the
admission is perhaps dangerous but the figure is
magnificent :—

By their own arts, 'tis righteously decreed,
Those dire artificers of death shall bleed.
Against themselves their witnesses will swear
Till, viper-like, their mother-plot they tear,
And suck for nutriment that bloody gore
Which was their principle of life before.
Their Belial with their Beelzebub will fight;
Thus on my foes my foes shall do me right.

(1010 ff.)

In Belial and Beelzebub we may see an allusion—
though but a vague and undefined allusion—to the
divisions among the fiends of the Second Book of
Paradise Lost, where Belial 'counselled ignoble
ease' (227) and Beelzebub advocated a 'bold design'
(386); similar touches—no more than touches—
sustain the satiric parts of the poem.

But Dryden's art is not confined to elevation ;
he is equally skilful in sinking his style when the
subject demands it.   One of the methods used is
the introduction of double rhymes, very rare in this
poem.   Double rhymes were associated with Butler's
Hudibras and with 'low satire.'   What Dryden's
opinion on the subject was, we learn from his *Discourse Concerning the Original and Progress of
Satire*, where he writes :—

> And besides, the double rhyme (a necessary companion
> of burlesque writing), is not so proper for manly satire ; for
> it turns earnest too much to jest, and gives us a boyish kind
> of pleasure.   It tickles awkwardly with a kind of pain, to the
> best sort of readers : we are pleased ungratefully, and, if I
> may say so, against our liking.

In *Absalom and Achitophel* the double rhyme is
used with effect in his satire on the fanatics of the
Commonwealth, the Levites, who stand for some
sort of clergy, and again in his description of Zimri
(Buckingham) :—

> Hot Levites headed these ; who pull'd before
> From the ark, which in the Judges' days they bore,
> Resum'd their cant, and with a zealous cry
> Pursu'd their old beloved theocracy,
> Where Sanhedrin and priest enslav'd the *nation*
> And justifi'd their spoils by *inspiration* ;
> For who so fit for reign as Aaron's race,
> If once dominion they could found in grace?   (519 ff.)

He says of Zimri :—

> Then all for women, painting, rhyming, *drinking*,
> Besides ten thousand freaks that died in *thinking*.
>
> (551 f.)

and again :—

> So over violent or over *civil*
> That every man with him was God or *Devil*.   (557 f.)

These are the only instances of double rhyme in the poem.

The admirable satire of the Opposition in general (491–540) is followed by the satiric portraits of individuals (541–681) of which the most important are Buckingham as Zimri, Slingsby Bethel as Shimei —types of the discontented noble and the city-man— and Oates as Corah, a supplement not to be left out; for though

> To speak the rest, who better are forgot,
> Would tire a well-breath'd witness of the plot.
> Yet, Corah, thou shalt from oblivion pass ;
> Erect thyself, thou monumental brass,
> High as the serpent of thy metal made,
> While nations stand secure beneath thy shade. (630 ff.)

The danger of this style is that the personal detail may be tiresome and obscure even at the moment of writing, and still more so for later generations. Dryden has not wholly avoided this danger.   The couplet, for instance, about 'canting Nadab' :—

> And canting Nadab let oblivion damn
> Who made new porridge for the paschal lamb.

is open to this objection, as well as to others, that the allusion is unintelligible without a lengthy note. Satire is apt to consist of such things as this, and it dies of them unless rescued by other merits.

The tone of Dryden's satiric piece is not indignation but contempt, and this feeling is consistent

with the whole poem, which is a celebration of the
King's triumph; Dryden, in fact, 'rebates the satire'
for the sake of 'sweetness.' He is at his best in the
general part, rather than in the portraits of individuals. Read, for instance, his description, already
quoted, of the 'hot Levites,' or Presbyterians (519 ff.),
of the 'enthusiastic breed' (529 ff.), representing the
Baptists and other Nonconformists; and especially
of the general mass of the English, obstinate in
Protestant prejudice because it is English :—

> But far more numerous was the herd of such
> Who think too little and who talk too much.
> These out of mere instinct, they knew not why,
> Ador'd their fathers' God and property,
> And by the same blind benefit of Fate
> The Devil and the Jebusite did hate :
> Born to be sav'd even in their own despite,
> Because they could not help believing right.   (533 ff.)

Note the sneer at the complacent acquiescence in
their local religion, 'their fathers' God.' Dryden
was indeed no true Anglican. This real feeling of
his comes out again in an earlier passage in the
poem where the distinctive historical claim of the
Jebusites, representing the Catholics, is emphasised
by the pause, due to the shortened line, unique in
this poem :—

> The inhabitants of old Jerusalem
> Were Jebusites; the town so call'd from them,
> And theirs the native right.
> But when the chosen people grew more strong,...
>
>   (85 ff.)

and there are many other marks of his feeling.

His conversion to Roman Catholicism can have come as no surprise to students of his works. To discuss Dryden's religious opinions however would take us too far from our present subject, and belongs more especially to the consideration of his two religious poems, *Religio Laici* and *The Hind and the Panther*[1]. But students interested in the question should read the chapter on Dryden's life from 1680 to 1688 in Mr Saintsbury's *Dryden*, published in 1881 in the series of *English Men of Letters*.

In the case of individual portraits Dryden felt the danger of over-elaboration and consequent obscurity, and was disposed to pass them over briefly. One exception is made in the case of the Sheriff of the City of London, Bethel (Shimei), who seems to have been not popular even with his own party, fanatic though he was; for he was stingy, 'not prodigal of pelf,' and showed no hospitality, in spite of the traditions of his office :—

> And that his noble style he might refine,
> No Rechabite more shunn'd the fumes of wine.
> Chaste were his cellars, and his shrieval board
> The grossness of a city feast abhorr'd :
> His cooks with long disuse their trade forgot ;
> Cool was his kitchen, though his brains were hot.
>
> (616 ff.)

The description is too long but has amusing points : the representation of moneyed men as 'dissenting Jews,' for instance, is unfair but smart, and the reference to the fire of London :—

[1] See below, p. 147.

> For towns once burnt such magistrates require
> As dare not tempt God's providence by fire.

is interesting, as discrediting the contemporary accusation against the Catholics of voluntary incendiarism.

Another exception to the brevity of these satiric portraits is made in the case of Oates (632–681). Oates is a figure difficult to omit, but he will not come within Dryden's general tone: Oates is no object for levity. Moreover it was known that the King meant to use the false witnesses against the Exclusionist party, a policy definitely announced in the passage from David's speech above quoted. Dryden however makes the most of the comic points in his description of Oates, his long and solemn face, his spurious D.D. degree; nor does he forget that he was a clergyman, and so one of a class of persons generally mischievous, according to Dryden. The best point in the account is the gay defiance of the personal touch—the single appearance in the poem of the author in his own person:—

> Were I myself in witness Corah's place,
> The wretch who did me such a dire disgrace
> Should whet my memory, though once forgot,
> To make him an appendix of my plot.   (668 ff.)

There is an odd touch in the phrase describing the Levites, or clergy :—

> His tribe were God Almighty's gentlemen

Here comes out the traditional dislike of the squire for the parson and his pretensions to an equality

with the country gentry; here speaks the nephew
of baronets—here, and often.

Then we pass (682–750) to Absalom's appeal
to the people, the organisation of his progresses
through the country, and the consolidation of the
party. The summary is very skilful. It is followed
(753–810) by a general argument for not disturbing
the traditional basis of government : there is no
security in speculation, as has been proved by recent
experience. This is the gravest part of the poem.
A prevalent theory of the time is here set out—
that the State is founded on an 'original contract'
between the King and the people, who have sur-
rendered their natural liberty in return for protection
from him. An illustration of this theory was afforded
less than eight years afterwards by the vote declaring
the throne vacant at the Revolution. Early in 1689,
the Convention Parliament resolved that James
'having endeavoured to subvert the constitution by
breaking the original contract between King and
people...had violated the fundamental laws...and
that the throne was vacant.'

Dryden assumes this position and shows its uncertain results : admit that 'people' (759) ought not
to bind their posterity absolutely, yet, in a contract, such a power of resumption should have been
declared. Was it ? And if Adam could bind his
posterity by his sin, why could not 'the people' bind
theirs by their engagement ? (It is an odd argument, but in the style of the time.) And, if a
necessity for resumption of the contract may exist,

who is to judge?   The multitude?   Or Parliament,
itself only a multitude after all ?—

> What standard is there in a fickle rout,
> Which, flowing to the mark, runs faster out?
> Nor only crowds but Sanhedrins may be
> Infected with this public lunacy,
> And share the madness of rebellious times,
> To murder monarchs for imagin'd crimes.   (785 ff.)

To diverge for the moment from the general
consideration of the argument, and deal with a particular point, I cannot accept Mr Churton Collins's
suggested explanation of the first couplet in the
above lines, which he calls 'very obscure.' He
thinks that 'the metaphor is from water which in
flowing to a mark, and so acquiring impetus, is by
its very impetus carried on and past—into waste.'
But how does water acquire impetus in flowing to
a mark, and what are we to understand by the
mark ?   The lines are perhaps obscure—a rare fault
in Dryden—but the metaphor is unmistakable : the
'mark' is the extreme high-water mark of a spring
tide, and Dryden observes, quite accurately, that the
higher the tide and consequently the greater the
distance between high and low water-mark (the interval of time between tides remaining the same),
the more rapid is the fall of the water at the ebb.
The words 'flowing,' 'mark,' and 'runs out' would
seem sufficient to indicate the metaphor, and all
doubt is removed by the allusion in the next lines to
another effect of the moon, mistress, in the opinion
of the time, alike of madness and of the tides.

To go back to Dryden's argument: whatever the theory of the relations between Crown and People, tradition is the only safety. As students of literature we need not criticise this view, but we should note the admirable summary in the concluding couplet :—

> The tampering world is subject to this curse,
> To physic their disease into a worse.

We next pass to an account of the loyalists, headed by Barzillai, who stands for Dryden's patron the Marquis, and soon afterwards Duke, of Ormond, and Lord Lieutenant of Ireland. In the reference to the recent death of his son, the Earl of Ossory, 'Heaven' is better managed by Dryden than usual :—

> Now, free from earth, thy disencumber'd soul
> Mounts up, and leaves behind the clouds and starry pole:
> From thence thy kindred legions mayest thou bring
> To aid the guardian angel of thy King.
> Here stop, my Muse, here cease thy painful flight;
> No pinions can pursue immortal height:
> Tell good Barzillai thou canst sing no more,
> And tell thy soul she should have fled before:
> Or fled she with his life, and left this verse
> To hang on her departed patron's hearse?   (850 ff.)

Then come the clergy, Sancroft, Archbishop of Canterbury, Compton, Bishop of London, whose 'noble stem' is not forgotten, and Dolben, whose former position as Dean of Westminster gives Dryden the opportunity for a compliment to his old school :—

> The Prophets' sons, by such example led,
> To learning and to loyalty were bred:
> For colleges on bounteous kings depend,
> And never rebel was to arts a friend.

Then follow Mulgrave (Adriel), 'the Muses' friend, himself a Muse,' Halifax (Jotham), who was not 'King's man' enough for Dryden, but the effect of his speech in the House of Lords against the Exclusion Bill is acknowledged: he

> then chose the better side,
> Nor chose alone, but turn'd the balance too,
> So much the weight of one brave man can do.

Laurence Hyde (Hushai) whose skill in finance is noted :—

> Tis easy conduct when exchequers flow,
> But hard the task to manage well the low.

and finally Sir Edward Seymour (Amiel). All were patrons of Dryden except this last named, formerly Speaker of the House of Commons—a position which according to Dryden he filled well—and afterwards very important as gaining the vote of the Moderates among the Tories in opposition to James II. Dryden apparently thought that Seymour had been undervalued, and does not forget that Seymour was the chief of the 'Squires,' 'of ancient race by birth...and without title great.' A Parliament of loyal Squires was probably Dryden's ideal. There is no allusion in the poem to Danby, who was nearer to Dryden as a politician than anyone. But at the time when the poem was published Danby was in prison and apparently ruined.

In a passage which deserves particular attention but is too long to quote (917–932) the Loyalists implore the King to stand firm. Note the syntax and construction which, at the end of their representations—enumerated, against normal English usage, in a series of anacoluthic sentences—produce on the reader the effect not of a conclusion, but only of a breathless pause; whereupon the King follows, as an oracle :—

> With all these loads of injuries opprest,
> And long revolving in his careful breast
> The event of things, at last his patience tir'd,   935
> Thus from his royal throne, by Heaven inspir'd,
> The godlike David spoke; with awful fear
> His train their Maker in their master hear.

Note also the overlapping in *v.* 935, with the resultant pause after the words 'the event of things,' and the break thus made before the final resolve to speak 'at last.' The sentiment expressed in the conclusion of this passage is not profanity or superstition. Dryden's point in speaking of 'their master' as 'their Maker' is that the people had not made royalty and the whole complex of which royalty was part, but, on the contrary, royalty had made them; they might as well say that they had made God. The feeling is strongly contrasted with that of the 'Adam-wits,' in an earlier passage :—

> Those very Jews who at their very best
> Their humour more than loyalty exprest,
> Now wondered why so long they had obey'd
> An idol monarch *which their hands had made;*

> Thought they might ruin him they could create
> Or melt him to that golden calf, a State.   (61 ff.)

—a State, in Dryden's language, meaning an arbitrary Commonwealth.

The King's speech—two passages of which I have already quoted—concludes with a peal of thunder, the stock epic ornament signifying divine approval and the nod of Heaven :—

> He said. The Almighty, nodding, gave consent;
> And peals of thunder shook the firmament.
> Henceforth a series of new time began,
> The mighty years in long procession ran ;
> Once more the god-like David was restor'd,
> And willing nations knew their lawful lord. (1026 ff.)

'Nodding' translates the Latin *nuere*, and the 'series of new time' and the 'mighty years' point to the King as the channel of divine counsel and decision by recalling the language of Virgil's Sibylline Eclogue :—

> Magnus ab integro saeclorum nascitur ordo.

IV

THE QUATRAIN POEMS

Stanzas on Oliver Cromwell, and *Annus Mirabilis*

Two poems of Dryden's are written in quatrains —stanzas that is, of four lines, with alternate rhymes —namely the *Heroic Stanzas Consecrated to the Memory of His Highness Oliver, late Lord Protector of this Commonwealth, etc.,* and *Annus Mirabilis; the Year of Wonders,* 1666.

In the Preface to *Annus Mirabilis* he tells us that he adopted the quatrain in that poem as being 'more noble and of greater dignity both for the sound and number than any other verse in use amongst us.' His praise is vague and opportunist, the quatrain having been used in *Gondibert* (published in 1651) by Davenant, with whom Dryden was at this time on intimate terms. The quatrain with its characteristic strong and frequent pauses and its slow and regular swing, is plainly unsuitable to narrative. It lends itself to reflexions, especially to detached reflexions, and is admirably adapted to its subject in the best and best known quatrain poem in English, Gray's *Elegy written in a Country Churchyard.* For Dryden's *Stanzas in Memory of Oliver,* 'written

after the celebrating of his funeral' and published in
1658, the metre is suitable enough; a good specimen is the final stanza :—

> His ashes in a peaceful urn shall rest;
>   His name a great example stands to show
> How strangely high endeavours may be blest
>   Where piety and valour jointly go.

There is merit also in other stanzas; take for
instance the first :—

> And now 'tis time; for their officious haste
>   Who would before have borne him to the sky,
> Like eager Romans, ere all rites were past,
>   Did let too soon the sacred eagle fly.

where the allusion, elsewhere[1] again introduced by
Dryden, is to the Roman custom of letting fly an
eagle upon the close of the funeral ceremonies of a
Roman Emperor.   Or take stanza 7 :—

> No borrow'd bays his temples did adorn,
>   But to our crown he did fresh jewels bring;
> Nor was his virtue poison'd, soon as born,
>   With the too early thoughts of being king.

These stanzas are mainly good, and so are parts of
stanzas 22–30; there is generosity and truth everywhere, yet the poem is not good as a whole.   There
is too much 'cockle' with the 'noble seed,' and
Dryden himself reminds us that the poetry written
before the Restoration did not provide the 'well-
winnow'd grain' commended in the *Threnodia
Augustalis*[2].

---

[1] *Tyrannic Love* IV 2.
[2] See above, p. 6.

There are faults of grammar :—

> When absent, yet we conquer'd in his right :   (24)

and of obscurity :—

> When such heroic virtue Heaven sets out,
> The stars, like Commons, sullenly obey,
> Because it drains them, when it comes about,
> And therefore is a tax they seldom pay.   (27)

And here, in addition to the obscurity, the first image, the soul from a starry Heaven, is degraded by the later comparison with Parliamentary supplies. This kind of fault, common in Dryden's predecessors, was very slowly eliminated from English poetry.

The poem supplies instances of artificial derangement of words :—

> And for him fiercely as for empire strove.   (22)

and of artificial choice of words :—

> And bravely fought where southern stars *arise*.   (31)

and

> The highest acts it could *produce to show*.   (32)

besides many others.   Points also are made without regard to their weight or real connexion, conceits being introduced merely for their own sakes, as in stanza 30, where the first good image :—

> That old unquestion'd pirate of the land
> Proud Rome

is followed by a dubious point in the third line, and a bad one in the last, thus :—

> And trembling wish'd behind more Alps to stand,
> Although an Alexander were her guard.

the contemporary Pope being Alexander VII !

The poem, however, is strong in expression and rich in fancy, and therein characteristic of Dryden. The special selection of Oliver's knowledge of men as a point for commendation is appropriate and finely expressed :—

> For from all tempers he could service draw;
>   The worth of each with its alloy he knew;
> And, as the confident of Nature, saw
>   How she complexions did divide and brew:
>
> Or he their single virtues did survey
>   By intuition in his own large breast,
> Where all the rich ideas of them lay
>   That were the rule and measure to the rest. (25, 26)

At a later time it suited Dryden's opponents to suppose an allusion to the execution of Charles I in the lines describing how Oliver

> fought to end our fighting, and assay'd
> To stanch the blood by breathing of the vein.   (12)

The suggestion is of course absurd, but, on the other hand, nowhere in the poem is there any enthusiasm for Oliver; the tone is one of sober admiration. Dryden remarks, at the opening, that the subject of his poem already holds so lofty a position that it cannot be raised by any 'arts' :—if only he had so reflected more often, and allowed his reflexions to determine his practice!

Does the poem prove that Dryden after the Restoration threw away all his principles? I think not. There is in it no praise of military government, nor any desire for its permanence.

Annus Mirabilis

Before the issue of the next quatrain poem, in 1667, Dryden had become a figure of some importance ; he had produced four or five dramas and written some court-poetry. The poem of *Annus Mirabilis* describes the events of that wonderful year 1666, when the plague and fire of London followed upon the naval war with the Dutch. It is preceded by an address to the City and a letter to Sir Robert Howard.

The address to the City is a fine piece of prose, and very characteristic of Dryden. Addressing the City of London he writes :—

> You are now a phoenix in her ashes, and, as far as humanity can approach, a great emblem of the suffering Deity. But Heaven never made so much piety and virtue to leave it miserable. I have heard indeed of some virtuous persons who have ended unfortunately, but never of any virtuous nation. Providence is engaged too deeply, when the cause becomes so general ; and I cannot imagine it has resolved the ruin of that people at home, which it has blessed abroad with such successes.

Note the Pagan feeling. There is no sense of mystery, and the Christian allusions are mere ornaments ; a comparison is made in the same breath of the City with the phoenix *and with Christ*. Man, he thinks, has a case against 'the gods' : 'Providence is engaged.' Dryden cannot see things big ; what he gives us is a poetic blend of conventional philosophy and religion.

In the *Letter to Sir Robert Howard* there is a deliberate challenge of criticism. This letter is throughout characteristic of Dryden. Not only does he, as we have seen, justify his choice of metre, but he has chosen 'the most heroic subject which any poet could desire,'—'incomparably the best subject,' he has ever had, 'excepting only the royal family.' The subject is indeed epic in dignity but the action is, as he admits, not 'properly one,' nor complete as a story. Dryden's whole ambition is disclosed in this Letter: to be high, like Virgil—who 'has been my master in this poem '—and yet real.

As regards his treatment of the metre, he tells us that he has discarded ancient licences :—

> Neither can we give ourselves the liberty of making any part of a verse for the sake of rhyme, or concluding with a word which is not current English, or using the variety of female rhymes; all which our fathers practised.

Dryden claims to have taken some trouble to introduce the 'proper terms' in his description of the naval fight. But are his terms altogether proper? Is, for instance, 'caulking-iron' correct? His criticism, a little later, of Ovid and Virgil has no substance, and though Virgil may have been his 'master' in this poem, Dryden is not at all like Virgil, and the resemblances quoted by him are insignificant: 'and lighted all the river with a blaze' (st. 231), for example, has but a slight resemblance to *Sigea igni freta lata relucent* (Virgil *Aen.* II 312). The language of the poem is current English, with a few innovations. To this point Dryden calls attention. But these innovations, introductions from Latin, were not efficient or numerous ; instances are :—

> With loathing eyes repeat what they would shun. (257)

where 'repeat' represents the Latin *repetere*, 'to seek again,' and

> By which to Heaven they did affect the way,   (273)

where 'affect' is used, as again in *Absalom and Achitophel* (178), in the sense of seeking or desiring; here it is probably an imitation of *viamque adfectat Olympo* (Virgil *Georgic* IV 562). We also have Latinisms in 'require' (st. 256) and 'obnoxious' (st. 258). His imitations of Latin models are not among his happiest passages : the bad lines

> And weary waves, withdrawing from the fight,
> Lie lulled and panting on the silent shore.   (98)

are, he tells us, reminiscent of Statius (*Silv.* v 4, 5):—

> Nec trucibus fluviis idem sonus; occidit horror
> aequoris, et terris maria adclinata quiescunt.

and his recent reading of the Third Book of Lucan's *Pharsalia*, where the successive ships are said to drive the sea's surface forward and back with their oars (III 550 ff.), has obviously suggested the hyperbolic language of stanza 177 :—

> So vast the navy now at anchor rides
> That underneath it the press'd waters fail,
> And with its weight it shoulders off the tides.

The success of the poem where Dryden treats of reality, of the actual, is yet uncommon. Take for instance the four stanzas (99–102) which describe the night before the third engagement of Albemarle's fleet with the Dutch. Albemarle's danger was great ; he was separated from Prince Rupert's detachment and had passed through two days of severe fighting against a force outnumbering his own. It is the night of June 2, the next day, June 3, being the anniversary of two earlier naval victories over the Dutch :—

> The moon shone clear on the becalmed flood,
> Where, while her beams like glittering silver play,
> Upon the deck our careful General stood,
> And deeply mus'd on the succeeding day.
>
> 'That happy sun,' said he, 'will rise again
> Who twice victorious did our navy see,
> And I alone must view him rise in vain,
> Without one ray of all his star for me.
>
> Yet like an English general will I die,
> And all the ocean make my spacious grave :
> Women and cowards on the land may lie ;
> The sea's a tomb that's proper for the brave.'
>
> Restless he pass'd the remnants of the night,
> Till the fresh air proclaim'd the morning nigh ;
> And burning ships, the martyrs of the fight,
> With paler fires beheld the eastern sky.

Dryden's vocabulary here is still that of current English, with the single exception, that since the complete separation of the services, the title 'General' is no longer satisfactory to our ears. But the separation had not been made in Dryden's time, and Monck, Duke of Albemarle, was indeed an English 'General' familiar enough to those who remembered that he had on a famous occasion ordered a change in the course of his ship by calling out, 'wheel to the left.'

With this successful description of a real situation should be contrasted Dryden's attempt at supernatural decoration in an earlier stanza :—

> To see this fleet upon the ocean move
>   Angels drew wide the curtains of the skies ;
> And Heaven, as if there wanted lights above,
>   For tapers made two glaring comets rise.   (16)

Dryden's 'Heaven' is the old *dome*, the concave covering of a circular flat earth.   His conception is affected by the example of Lucan, recently in his thoughts, as is shown by his reference to 'the third of his *Pharsalia*' in his *Letter to Sir Robert Howard*. In the Fourth Book of the *Pharsalia* (72 ff.) Lucan describes how the bad weather in Spain was caused by compression of the atmosphere, the westward driven air being unable to escape.   The conception of the sky as an inverted bowl resting upon the earth was not dead in antiquity, but was quite dead to Dryden, as is shown elsewhere and especially in the speculations, which follow in the very next stanzas, as to the nature of the 'two glaring comets' :—

> Whether they unctuous exhalations are
>   Fir'd by the sun, or seeming so alone,
> Or each some more remote and slippery star
>   Which loses footing when to mortals shown ;
>
> Or one that bright companion of the sun,
>   Whose glorious aspect seal'd our new-born King,
> And now, a round of greater years begun,
>   New influence from his walks of light did bring.

These speculations show some scientific knowledge of comets, extending beyond that of his ancient

models, but yet Dryden could not accept the true
astronomy. This confusion of astronomical conceptions comes out strongly in the stanza immediately
preceding his address to the Royal Society, of which
he had been elected a member some five years
earlier :—

> Then we upon our globe's last verge shall go
> And view the ocean leaning on the sky:
> From thence our rolling neighbours we shall know
> And on the lunar world securely pry[1].   (164)

The examination of Dryden's ' Heaven' well repays
a student of his works : it plays an important part,
and is always mischievous.

Between the Natural and the Supernatural is the
middle way of supernatural *machinery*. Here he
has better success. With good effect, in spite of the
flatness of the last line, the ghosts of men are introduced as interested spectators of the naval fight :—

> The mighty ghosts of our great Harrys rose,
> And armed Edwards looked with anxious eyes,
> To see this fleet among unequal foes,
> By which Fate promis'd them their Charles should rise,
> (81)

and again during the fire of London :—

> The ghosts of traitors from the Bridge descend,
> With bold fanatic spectres to rejoice;
> About the fire into a dance they bend
> And sing their sabbath notes with feeble voice. (223)

[1] For further comment on this stanza, as well as general
criticism of Dryden's work, the reader is referred to Lowell's
Essay on Dryden, contained in the volume called *My Study
Windows*.

But this method is not applicable on a large scale. Dryden's general tone is so positive and definite that the reader is tempted to ask, How did the ghosts come there? The spirits of Henri IV of France and William the Silent are, he lets us know, among 'the blessed,' the abode of 'the blessed' being a vague combination of the Christian Heaven and the ancient Elysium.

Dryden never succeeded in this way, he used no free invention. What he writes in the Preface to *Tyrannic Love* is generally true of his work in this kind :—

> As for what I have said of astral or aerial spirits, it is no invention of mine, but taken from those who have written on that subject. Whether there are such beings or not, it concerns not me; it is sufficient for my purpose, that many have believed the affirmative; and that these heroic representations, which are of the same nature with the epic, are not limited, but with the extremest bounds of what is credible.

In view of such an attitude success was hardly to be anticipated.

With this comparative failure we may contrast his success in natural imagination, and his admirable application of it to simile and metaphor. His faculty of imagination was strong, apt even to overleap its proper bounds. Of this Dryden was himself conscious. More than once he compares the faculty to a shooting-dog or spaniel; thus, in the Preface to *Annus Mirabilis*, he writes :—

> The faculty of imagination...like a nimble spaniel, beats over and ranges through the field of memory, till it springs the quarry it hunted after.

This 'spaniel' of his requires a check; and such a check is provided by rhyme, which needs reflexion. In the dedication of the *Rival Ladies* (published 1664) he had written that the chief benefit to be derived from rhyme is

> that it bounds and circumscribes the fancy. For imagi-
> nation in a poet is a faculty so wild and lawless, that, like an
> high-ranging spaniel, it must have clogs tied to it, lest it
> outrun the judgement. The great easiness of blank verse
> renders the poet too luxuriant;...but when the difficulty of
> artful rhyming is interposed...the fancy then gives leisure to
> the judgement to come in.

This faculty of his is not sufficient in itself for the highest work, but within its range it is excellent, especially when applied to the creation of metaphors and similes.

Of simile many good specimens are to be found in the *Annus Mirabilis*; as, for instance, the dog and hare, applied to the pursuing ship and the pursued, both alike disabled :—

> So have I seen some fearful hare maintain
>   A course, till tir'd before the dog she lay,
> Who, stretch'd behind her, pants upon the plain,
>   Past power to kill as she to get away:
> With his loll'd tongue he faintly licks his prey;
>   His warm breath blows her flix up as she lies;
> She, trembling, creeps upon the ground away,
>   And looks back to him with beseeching eyes.
>
> (131, 132)

Again, the falcon and crow :—

> Have you not seen when, whistled from the fist,
>   Some falcon stoops at what her eye design'd,
> And, with her eagerness the quarry miss'd,
>   Straight flies at check and clips it down the wind;

> The dastard crow, that to the wood made wing
>   And sees the groves no shelter can afford,
> With her loud caws her craven kind does bring,
>   Who, safe in numbers, cuff the noble bird. (86, 87)

Or the spider :—

> So the false spider, when her nets are spread,
>   Deep ambush'd in her silent den does lie,
> And feels far off the trembling of her thread,
>   Whose filmy cord should bind the struggling fly;
>
> Then, if at last she find him fast beset,
>   She issues forth and runs along her loom:
> She joys to touch the captive in her net
>   And drags the little wretch in triumph home.
>   (180, 181)

In the simile of the bees he is misled as to the facts by Virgil, whom he is consciously imitating :—

> All hands employ'd, the royal work grows warm;
>   Like labouring bees on a long summer's day,
> Some sound the trumpet for the rest to swarm,
>   And some on bells of tasted lilies play;
>
> With glewy wax some new foundation lay
>   Of virgin-combs, which from the roof are hung;
> Some arm'd within doors upon duty stay
>   Or tend the sick or educate the young. (144, 145)

And in the simile of the gold in mines ripened by the sun, he is misled by the science of his day :—

> As those who unripe veins in mines explore
>   On the rich bed again the warm turf lay,
> Till time digests the yet imperfect ore,
>   And know it will be gold another day.   (139)

One more illustration must suffice, that of the martlet whose wet wings bring the first news of the coming rain to the birds of lower flight :—

> As in a drought the thirsty creatures cry
>   And gape upon the gather'd clouds for rain,
> And first the martlet meets it in the sky,
>   And with wet wings joys all the feather'd train.   (110)

Here imagination seems to have outrun observation, but the simile is pleasing.

Even in natural figures the 'spaniel' sometimes ranges too high ; as, for instance, in the comparison of the small squadron surrounded by a larger squadron to the swordfish and the whale :—

> Our little fleet was now engag'd so far
>   That like the sword-fish in the whale they fought;
> The combat only seem'd a civil war,
>   Till through their bowels we our passage wrought.   (79)

The reader will notice in Dryden's work a certain coldness of emotion ; imagination is with him detached from feeling, as in the often quoted line describing the result of an attack upon the richly laden Dutch ships :—

> Some preciously by shatter'd porcelain fall
>   And some by aromatic splinters die.   (29)

More than one explanation can be found for this bluntness of feeling. It is partly due to the actual barbarian survivals of the time. Traitors' heads were exposed on London Bridge, and in the conclusion of Dryden's opera of *Albion and Albanius* there was a representation upon the stage of Shaftesbury's 'tap'—an appliance rendered necessary by a physical infirmity. It is also partly due to an ungoverned passionate curiosity for fact, common to the age, and specially characteristic of Dryden. But it is in the main inherited (and not yet worked off) from

Shakespeare and the Jacobeans generally; cold horror, however, has become more repulsive with increased precision of style and expression.

Dryden's figures in *Annus Mirabilis* are sometimes, but not commonly, mere conceits. Thus, in stanza 178 :—

> A breeze from westward waits their sails to fill
> And *rests* in those high *beds* his *downy* wings.

But such false points are rare.

If we examine in detail the images applied by Dryden to the supernatural we shall be struck by the concrete and material conception of the 'otherworld' which they exhibit. His antique and Pagan 'Heaven,' or sky, has been already noticed, but it does not stand alone. This material and concrete view is partly of the age or inherited from predecessors—Donne, for instance, and Herbert[1]—but it

---

[1] See, for instance, Herbert *The Holy Communion* (second poem) :—

> Before that sin turn'd flesh to stone,
> And all our lump to leaven,
> A fervent sigh might well have blown
> Our innocent earth to Heaven.

> For sure when Adam did not know
> To sin, or sin to smother,
> He might to Heaven from Paradise go
> As from one room t' another.

Or *Whitsunday* :—

> Such glorious gifts Thou didst bestow,
> That th' earth did like a Heaven appear:
> The stars were coming down to know
> If they might mend their wages, and serve here.

And Donne, *Ascension* :—

> O strong Ram, which hast batter'd Heaven for me.
> Mild Lamb, which with Thy Blood hath mark'd the path!

was congenial to Dryden's positive mind. He took religion as he found it, without much interest in it during the middle years of his life, and it is rare to find in him any sense of mystery,

An interesting illustration of his attitude is furnished by stanzas 209–211, where he makes the transition between the two subjects of his poem, passing from the naval victories to the fire of London :—

> But ah! how unsincere are all our joys,
>   Which sent from Heaven, like lightning, make no stay!
> Their palling taste the journey's length destroys,
>   Or grief sent post o'ertakes them on the way.
>
> Swell'd with our late successes on the foe,
>   Which France and Holland wanted power to cross,
> We urge an unseen fate to lay us low
>   And feed their envious eyes with English loss.
>
> Each element His dread command obeys
>   Who makes or ruins with a smile or frown ;
> Who as by one He did our nation raise,
>   So now He with another pulls us down.

The nation, that is, blessed by one element, water, is ruined by another, fire. Dryden here clearly does not mean any irreverence, and yet, look at the grotesque imagery of the first of these stanzas, with its suggestive reminiscences of the deterioration of vegetables and foreign groceries on their way between London and Charlton, where Dryden was writing ; the joys from Heaven are compared to spoilt provisions, and the passage to Heaven is a long post-stage! In the intermediate stanza we may note the introduction of the pagan idea of Nemesis,

the jealous fate that overtakes prosperity. This
Dryden would have considered an established figure,
independent of any actual belief in such a power.
But the introduction of Nemesis here is nevertheless chilling to a spiritual imagination.

Somewhat similar is his conception of the limited
and anthropomorphic Deity. His concrete imagination extends from mystery itself to acts of mystery,
such, for instance, as the Creation, and this attitude
is especially common in his treatment of kings in
general and the King in especial. Kings are to him
earthly Gods. The view is partly living and political, derived from his sense of the importance of
monarchy—his politics we discuss elsewhere[1]—partly
literary, due to his study of the Roman poets, Virgil,
Horace, Ovid, and others, with their feeling for
the worship and religion of the Roman Emperor.
A specimen of this attitude is found in the stanzas
where he is describing how Charles orders the repair
of the fleet after the 'Four Days Battle.' The King's
external relation to the successive stages of the war
is compared to the Creator's relation to the days
of creation :—

> So looks our Monarch on this early fight,
>   The essay and rudiments of great success,
> Which all-maturing time must bring to light,
>   While he, like Heaven, does each day's labour bless.
>
> Heaven ended not the first or second day,
>   Yet each was perfect to the work design'd :
> God and kings work, when they their work survey,
>   And passive aptness in all subjects find.   (140, 141)

[1] See above, pp. 19 ff., 49 ff.

This is not personal servility or adulation. The poet feels the greatness of obedience and of a coherent frame ; the greatest thing we see is compared to the greatest that we know—the universe. But the cold and unmysterious imagination degrades it.

Somewhat similar objections have been felt to Dryden's treatment of Old Testament stories, but these stories are not always spiritual, and Dryden seems to me sound in instinct here. Take, for instance, the touching of the ark, in stanza 94. During Albemarle's retreat after the second day's battle one of the pursuing ships was unexpectedly sunk. The fortune seemed miraculous, and Dryden writes :—

> The foe approach'd ; and one for his bold sin
> Was sunk, as he that touch'd the Ark was slain.

Scott calls this profane. I do not feel it so, and at all events, we may welcome the fine figure which follows :—

> The wild waves master'd him, and suck'd him in,
> And smiling eddies dimpled on the main.

The politics of the *Annus Mirabilis* are out of date. It is largely coloured by animosity against the Dutch ; the Dutch figure, for instance, is a subject of attack :—

> Vast bulks, which little souls but ill supply.   (70)

Dryden's materialism here is antique ; he is thinking of soul as soul-substance, not as immaterial spirit. But even so the allusion is to us somewhat coarse,

and again here, as so often, there is too familiar a
handling of mystery. Such formations—vast bodies
with little souls—are according to him specially liable
to nightmare! and there follows a splendid description of nightmare :—

> In dreams they fearful precipices tread,
> Or shipwrack'd labour to some distant shore,
> Or in dark churches walk among the dead ;
> They wake with horror and dare sleep no more. (71)

Dryden is not insensible to the pathos of war,
and gives his compassion to Dutch sufferers in
four stanzas (32–35) marked by good taste. He
supposes some Dutch merchant-vessels from the
east to have been captured by the English, a likely
enough incident. Pure reality is Dryden's strength,
and elegiac meditation is suitable to his chosen
metre :—

> Go, mortals, now and vex yourselves in vain
> For wealth, which so uncertainly must come ;
> When what was brought so far and with such pain
> Was only kept to lose it nearer home.

> The son who, twice three months on the ocean tost,
> Prepar'd to tell what he had pass'd before,
> Now sees in English ships the Holland coast
> And parents' arms in vain stretch'd from the shore.

> This careful husband had been long away
> Whom his chaste wife and little children mourn,
> Who on their fingers learn'd to tell the day
> On which their father promis'd to return.

> Such are the proud designs of human kind,
> And so we suffer shipwrack everywhere !
> Alas, what port can such a pilot find
> Who in the night of Fate must blindly steer !

To understand Dryden's attitude in the poem, we must realise what was the contemporary conception of the European situation. England had been mistaken in the policy pursued from the days of Elizabeth to those of Oliver, the policy of depressing Spain and raising Holland and France, more dangerous enemies. Both these countries were ungrateful for English aid rendered in the past, and so Dryden, writing of the second battle on July 25, St James's Day, says :—

> Or if too busily they will enquire
>   Into a victory which we disdain,
> Then let them know the Belgians did retire
>   Before the patron saint of injur'd Spain.
>
> Repenting England, this revengeful day,
>   To Philip's manes did an offering bring,
> England, which first by leading them astray
>   Hatch'd up rebellion to destroy her King.
>
> Our fathers bent their baneful industry
>   To check a monarchy that slowly grew,
> But did not France or Holland's fate foresee,
>   Whose rising power to swift dominion flew.   (197 ff.)

And then former Dutch and French statesmen are represented as disapproving the conduct of their ungrateful successors :—

> But whate'er English to the blest shall go,
>   And the fourth Harry or first Orange meet,
> Find him disowning of a Bourbon foe
>   And him detesting a Batavian fleet.   (201)

This stanza has been ill explained. Scott says—and Christie takes the same view—that William the Silent repents his rebellion against Spain, and Henri IV his wars in France, as having encouraged rebellion generally and especially in England. The first of these explanations is irrelevant, and the second inconsistent with the words 'Bourbon foe.' The opponents of Henri IV were not Bourbons, but of the House of Valois; the Bourbon dynasty came in with Henri IV. The 'Bourbon foe' of this stanza is Louis XIV, disowned by Henri IV his grandfather, as a foe to the English[1]. William the Silent, the 'first Orange,' detests the fleet of Holland as employed against his benefactors. The point is worth notice because Dryden is rarely obscure.

We pass to the second portion of the poem, the Fire of London. The transition to this from the naval victories has been described above. An early stanza in the account of the fire will remind the reader, both in subject and metrical form, of Gray's famous line, 'Some Cromwell guiltless of his country's blood.' Dryden's stanza runs :—

> As when some dire usurper Heaven provides
> To scourge his country with a lawless sway;
> His birth perhaps some petty village hides
> And sets his cradle out of Fortune's way;   (213)

In the preceding stanza we have a comparison to the Day of Judgement; the fate of London is

[1] The above note was written in 1911, in ignorance that the same explanation of this passage had been made a year earlier by Mr G. C. Macaulay (*Mod. Lang. Review*, Vol. v, p. 234).

> Great as the world's, which at the death of time
> 　Must fall, and rise a nobler frame by fire.

Dryden's imagination was always haunted by the Day of Judgement. It appears and re-appears in his work. Criticism of his treatment might be multiplied, but it is enough here to set beside the lines just quoted—reminiscent, as Dryden tells us, of a passage in the *Metamorphoses* of Ovid (VII 453)— the naive representation of contemporary belief in a later stanza :—

> Night came, but without darkness or repose,
> 　A dismal picture of the general doom ;
> Where souls distracted, when the trumpet blows,
> 　And half unready with their bodies come.　(254)

This part of the poem contains an abundance of fine lines and passages ; take for instance the three stanzas beginning with the following :—

> The diligence of trades, and noiseful gain,
> 　And luxury, more late, asleep were laid ;
> All was the Night's, and in her silent reign
> 　No sound the rest of Nature did invade.　(216)

Or again the nine stanzas of the King's prayer, too long to quote here, beginning :—

> 'O God' said he, 'Thou patron of my days,
> 　Guide of my youth in exile and distress !
> Who me unfriended broughtst by wondrous ways,
> 　The kingdom of my fathers to possess.'　(262)

The supernatural imagination in this part of the poem is perhaps more successful than usual. The description in stanzas 279 and 280 oddly anticipates (with a difference) Milton's description in the Third

Book of *Paradise Lost*, published a few months later. There too, in the 'Empyrean,' surrounded by 'thrones' and 'dominions,' the Almighty contemplates a burning world, from whose ashes a new earth shall arise. Here,

> In the empyrean Heaven, the blest abode,
>   The thrones and the dominions prostrate lie,
> Not daring to behold their angry God;
>   And a hush'd silence damps the tuneful sky.
>
> At length the Almighty cast a pitying eye,
>   And mercy softly touch'd His melting breast;
> He saw the town's one half in rubbish lie
>   And eager flames give on to storm the rest.

Then, after describing the 'hollow crystal pyramid' with which the Almighty extinguished the flames, Dryden tells us that

> Each household Genius shows again his face
> And from the hearths the little Lares creep.

The introduction of Roman mythology into the midst of the scriptural imagery is more surprising to the modern reader than to Dryden's contemporaries. Bacchus and Christ both appear, for instance, in the opening Canto of Camoens' Portuguese epic, the *Lusiad*, of which the first English translation, by Fanshawe, had appeared in 1665, and Milton himself in *Paradise Lost* converts the Pagan gods into fiends (*P.L.* 1 437–521).

The same intermingling of disparate supernatural elements occurs in the allusion to the destruction of St Paul's, which perished, Dryden tells us, though it was dedicated to God and had been celebrated

by Waller on the occasion of its reparation by
Charles I :—

> Nor could thy fabric, Paul's, defend thee long,
> Though thou wert sacred to thy Maker's praise,
> Though made immortal by a poet's song,
> And poets' songs the Theban walls could raise. (275)

The technical execution of the whole poem is
excellent, and shows a marked advance on the
earlier quatrain poem. Forced rhyme, for instance,
is almost unknown. There is one example in the
unusual sense given to the word 'doom' (st. 207),
suggesting that it has been brought in, amid the
prosy details of stanzas 206, 207, for the rhyme with
'loom,' and possibly a similar reason accounts for
the unusual meaning of 'succeed,' in the sense of
'make to succeed' in stanza 292, though the word
is used in the same sense elsewhere by Dryden.
Weak rhymes are very rare ; 'murderer' rhyming
with 'appear' is an almost solitary instance and
Dryden is seldom contented even with such generally recognised rhymes as 'destiny' with 'shall be'
(st. 200), or 'industry' with 'foresee' in stanza 199,
quoted above.

One dubious case there is where the rhyme in
the last line seems forced on a first reading, but a
change in punctuation would remedy this by giving
a point to the rhyming word. Dryden is pro-
phesying the development of the new 'Augusta
Londiniensis' which is to be built in the place
of the old London which the fire had destroyed.

The stanza as commonly punctuated runs as follows :—

> More great than human now and more August,
>   New deified she from her fires does rise:
> Her widening streets on new foundations trust,
>   And, opening, into larger parts she flies.   (295)

If, however, we punctuate the last line thus, 'And opening into larger parts,—she flies,' the last word gains a meaning in the comparison of the city to a 'deified' Heracles, purged by burning, rarified, and so more able to ascend the sky. With the quotation of the two beautiful stanzas next following we conclude our examination of the poem :—

> Before, she like some shepherdess did show
>   Who sate to bathe her by a river's side,
> Not answering to her fame, but rude and low,
>   Nor taught the beauteous arts of modern pride.

> Now like a maiden queen she will behold
>   From her high turrets hourly suitors come;
> The East with incense and the West with gold
>   Will stand like suppliants to receive her doom.

>   (296, 297)

V

LITERARY CRITICISM IN THE AGE OF DRYDEN:
THE 'UNITIES'; THE *ESSAY OF DRAMATIC
POESY*

I

*Reason for discussing the 'Unities of Aristotle'
in connexion with Dryden*

DRYDEN'S prose works are mainly critical, and
are largely concerned with dramatic criticism, a very
considerable part of his prose writings being in the
form of Prefaces to plays or poems, dedications, and
so on. The most attractive perhaps are *An Essay
of Dramatic Poesy* (1668), its sequel *The Defence of
an Essay of Dramatic Poesy*, and—the work of his
last days—the Preface to the volume called *Fables*,
published in 1700. These are all included in the two
volumes of Professor Ker's selection of Dryden's
prose works (*Essays of John Dryden*), a book indis-
pensable to students. The two first are full of the
current contemporary discussion of the dramatic
rule of the 'Unities' as propounded by French
critics—Bossu, Rapin, and others—and more or
less acknowledged and obeyed by Corneille. Some
understanding of the contemporary view is therefore

necessary to readers of Dryden.   Moreover the subject itself is most curious as affording a specimen alike of the development of a theory and of the strange working of the human mind—the obstinate persistence of errors once made, and the extreme difficulty of retracing steps.

No complete statement on the matter, however, is to be found.   The assumption of the sixteenth and seventeenth century critics is that the 'rule of the Unities' is to be found, not textually but in substance, in Aristotle's *Poetics*, which is a treatise on tragedy, and in Horace's *Ars Poetica*; and further they assume that the rules were observed in practice by the ancient tragedians, notably by Sophocles and Euripides, from observation and criticism of whom Aristotle drew his principles[1].

Now all this is untrue.   The theory of the 'Unities' is a mere piece of confusion, arising from a false attempt to justify supposed ancient practices which, *so far as they existed*, had a totally different origin.   But these facts are nowhere clearly given. Commentaries on Aristotle and on ancient drama are indifferent to the theory of the 'Unities'—by which here and always I mean the Renaissance

[1] It is just, however, in speaking of the Renaissance criticism, to draw a certain distinction in favour of the earlier Italians. These understood Aristotle far better, and represented his opinions, both on this and on other matters, with far greater fidelity than their followers.   The doctrine of the Unities was not fully formulated until nearly the end of the sixteenth century, and it was afterwards developed on French rather than on Italian soil.

doctrine—and students of the Renaissance are little concerned with the ancients. Professor Ker, for instance, in his edition of Dryden's Essays, is excellent and full in reference on the Renaissance view, but says nothing of the ancient practice. Nor does he give material for estimating the value of what Dryden says about 'the ancients,' outrageous statements by Dryden being passed in silence; and it is the same with other editors.

The subject is one with which I have myself partly dealt in an essay on the Unity of Time appended to an edition of the *Ion* of Euripides (Introduction, pp. xlviii ff.) but that book is perhaps not easily accessible, the essay does not deal with the matter completely, and it is not specially adapted to students of Dryden.

2

The practice of the Athenian tragedians

We must begin by asking, What was the practice, so far as relevant to our purpose, of the ancient Athenian tragic poets. An integral part of their stage-machinery, quite unrepresented in ours, was the Chorus, a body of performers singing and accompanying their song by symmetrical movements or figures, generally pairs of figures—that is, the same figure danced twice. The number of performers in the tragic Chorus was eventually fifteen.

Greek tragedy was originally choric, what we call drama—that is to say, dialogue—being an addition.

The single performer of the earlier days, who conversed with the leader of the Chorus, had developed at the great period of Greek drama into three actors, and between the scenes of dialogue, the Chorus performed choric movements accompanied by songs expressing or commenting on the dramatic situation. A broad difference between the scenes and the choric interludes was made by the metre used : the scenes of dialogue were written in a simple metre resembling our blank verse, while the choric figures and corresponding metres were highly elaborate and various. There was also a difference in the language used in the two parts, besides other differences which we may pass, only noting generally that between the dialogue-scenes and the interludes there was a broad unmistakable distinction, corresponding with the difference of their nature. To put it briefly, the scenes were dramatic, in our sense of the word, and the interludes were not.

Between the successive scenes there would naturally be, and is, a *supposed* interval of time, sufficient to cover some necessary intermediate action ;—as for instance, while some one consults an oracle, while an assembly is held, while a battle is fought, while a messenger goes and returns, etc., etc. These intervals are of various length, defined sufficiently by the dialogue-scenes and by the natural relation of scene to scene.

These *supposed* intervals or lapses of time, are represented by the choric interludes, which were very suitable for the purpose, inasmuch as the nature of the choric performances was not dramatic. Song is sung and figure danced, and, prompted by this interruption of the action, we *suppose* the lapse of time, for which the previous scene has prepared us and which the following scene assumes. Thus, the choric interludes play the part of our drop-scene or curtain. Probably no curtain was used by Aeschylus, Sophocles and Euripides, but this point we need not here investigate; the choric interlude is equivalent to the curtain of the modern theatre.

Note also that the Chorus, the fifteen performers so called, were, after their original entry, on the scene throughout. They represented such bodies as councillors (of a king), visitors (of a woman in distress), and so on. Their main function in developed tragedy was to sing and perform the interludes, for which purpose they largely dropped their character; but their leader, and sometimes others, also took part in the scene-dialogue.

Now the question arises: Did this method of exhibiting stories in action impose any restriction on the choice and shape of the story or action which should be represented?

Let us clear this question. A *narrative* is obviously unlimited (*a*) in respect of the time covered, which may, for instance, be a whole reign, a life, the rise and fall of the Roman Empire, the world from *Genesis* to the Day of Judgement; and (*b*) in changes of place. *Dramatic representation* makes in theory no difference. There would be no difficulty in representing the reign of Victoria by successive scenes distributed over the time covered—such as the Coronation, the Queen's Marriage, the Russian War, the Indian Mutiny, the death of the Prince Consort, the Queen's Proclamation as Empress of India, and the Boer War—the supposed place varying accordingly, while the lapses of time were covered by lowering a drop-scene. Shakespeare's historical plays are instances in point, and in *The Winter's Tale* there is a gap of a whole generation. Were then the Athenians, with their choric method of performance, equally free ?

In theory perhaps they were. It would be possible to have a Chorus, whether silent or speaking in the scenes, marking each division of the scenes by a choric song. In some such fashion, in Shakespeare's *Henry V*, the Chorus, admitted 'to this history,' is present throughout, and delivers a *Prologue* to each Act and the *Epilogue* to the whole. And we are told by Aristotle (*Poetics* v) that originally the same freedom of time-limit was admitted in Greek tragedy as in epic poetry.

But practically it was not so. Let us take a modern illustration and suppose that the 'Reign of Victoria' is to be represented in this fashion. Our Chorus is to be present at the Coronation, the Indian Mutiny, and the Jubilee, taking part in each event. How could this fail to strike the audience as unnatural and absurd ? Further how could the Chorus, the same persons, be at a scene of the Indian Mutiny, and at a scene of the Boer War ? Thus the existence of the Chorus imposes a practical restriction both on the total time covered by the story and on the variation of its place.

First as to ' Time.' The restriction on the total of the supposed time is not definable but is manifestly narrow: the scenes have to be all such and so related that the same body of subordinate personages could be fairly supposed present at all. Such a condition is really impossible, nor did the Athenians really fulfil it ; when the stage convention was thoroughly established, unnatural choruses—the presence, that is, of persons unlikely in fact to be there—came to be ignored. But the smaller the total time covered by the action, the less apparent the break with nature. No actual rule was ever laid down, so far as we know, but in practice the total time did not usually exceed a 'day' (taken loosely) with some invasion of the preceding or succeeding night. Consideration will show that this was the natural practical outcome.

There was then no rule, nor was there any absolute uniformity of practice. Aeschylus, being earlier in manner, is not for this purpose representative, as in his day the practice was hardly established. But look at Euripides' play *The Suppliants*, written late in the classical century, say about 420 B.C. In that play there is a gap in the action which must allow for the raising of an army at Athens, its march to Thebes, and its triumph and return, altogether a period of ten days or more ; the total time of the play therefore includes and exceeds this period. The gap is conventionally represented in the usual

way by a choric song, equivalent to our curtain.
The scenes preceding and following the gap are at
the same place, namely, beside an altar, where the
Chorus is supposed to be found again after the interval. The circumstances are fairly favourable to this
arrangement, but it is rather a strain upon the imagination of the audience.

Now observe : there is no pretence or suggestion
in Euripides' *Suppliants* that the action is comprised
in a day ; it manifestly is not, but contains a gap of
ten days. The facts supposed are as clear as in
The Winter's Tale or any modern play—only the
gap is less conveniently represented, and in such a
way that an element not very natural is introduced
into adjacent scenes, namely, the presence in each
of the Chorus. In this there is no absurdity, no
obscurity ; only, I repeat, a certain inconvenience.
This inconvenience is generally avoided by the Greek
tragedians, in spite of the inconvenience, in another
way, of an action limited to 'a day.'

Next as to 'Place.' Here restriction was inevitable ; a shift of scene meant a supposed move of
the Chorus, and a move of the Chorus is open to
more than one objection : it is difficult to justify in
the action, and it leaves the scene empty, an awkward
thing where there is no curtain. Numerous moves
would result in a grotesque effect, like that deliberately intended by the moving about Paris of the
wedding party in Labiche's play, *Le Chapeau de
Paille d'Italie*. Thus under the conditions of Greek
drama a change of scene was not in itself desirable,

and the simplicity of Greek scenery perhaps further commended the Athenian usage. There was, however, no rule nor any uniformity of observance. In the *Ajax* of Sophocles, for instance, the scene changes some half-way through the play from the ground before the tent of Ajax to a lonely spot on the seashore, and the Chorus makes a second entry. But in the general practice there was identity of place in all the scenes.

Lastly, these practical restrictions of time and place tended perhaps to reinforce a universal rule or prescription, common to good narrative as to good drama—namely, that all the scenes told or shown should illustrate *the theme* of the story. If you narrate or show a scene which might, it is true, occur in the series, but which throws no light on the story, you distract attention and obscure your purpose. Athenian tragedy was less tempted to ignore this principle, because, with a narrow limit to the supposed time of action and with identity of place, there was no room for excrescences. It was hard enough to get in all that was relevant and necessary. The extant tragic poets almost never offend in this way, though some tragedians, so Aristotle tells us, did so offend (*Poetics* IX 10).

The Athenian tragic practice, which I have been shortly describing, is surely quite simple, clear, and natural in the circumstances. Ancient Comedy I will not touch, among other reasons for these two: our examples are deficient, and Aristotle's treatise is confined to Tragedy. I only note that, though in the Later Comedy there was no Chorus, the tragic precedent seems to have restricted possible liberties. But our information on this subject is defective and our inferences must be uncertain.

3

Aristotle's 'Poetics'

About a century later than the great age of Greek tragedy Aristotle wrote the *Poetics*, which is a theory of tragedy based on observation and on criticism of the classical practice, mainly the practice of Sophocles and Euripides; the work is, however, incomplete, confused, and often obscure. Let us examine what Aristotle says of our three topics, (1) limitation of supposed time, (2) identity of supposed place, (3) relevance of the separate scenes to the general theme of the story. Does he on these matters give any precept?

(1) Limitation of the total supposed time he notes *as a fact of practice*: 'Tragedy endeavours, as far as possible, to confine itself to a single revolution of the sun, or but slightly to exceed this limit[1]' (*Poet.* v 4). It is to be observed that Aristotle does not give any opinion upon the practice, which he neither commends nor blames. Probably he perceived the truth, that the limitation was inconvenient, but for the Athenian or Choric form of tragedy practically necessary; and it is noteworthy that

---

[1] Here and throughout the translation used is that of Professor Butcher in *Aristotle's Theory of Poetry and Fine Art.*

he expressly keeps open the question whether the Athenian form is the best and ultimate form of tragedy. He takes that form as a *datum*. (*Poet.* IV 11). Nor does he explain the grounds of this practice of time-limitation, but simply states it as a fact and leaves it.

(2) About the identity of the supposed place he says nothing at all. If he had, he would probably have treated it, like the limitation of time, as a fact of practice. But he says nothing about it. Some Renaissance critics notice this omission, and Dryden, in the person of Eugenius, in the *Essay of Dramatic Poesy*, mentions it :—

> But in the first place give me leave to tell you, that the Unity of Place, however it might be practised by them, was never any of their rules: we neither find it in Aristotle, Horace, or any who have written of it, till in our age the French poets first made it a precept of the stage.

(3) About the relevance of scenes he is, on the other hand, explicit and emphatic. His word for scenes is 'episodes' (*epeisodia*). From this he coins an adjective (*epeisodiodes*, i.e. 'epeisodic') to describe a play in which the scenes, or some of them, have no connexion of relevance to a common theme, scenes of which you can only say that such a series *might* occur in nature, though there is no reason why it should, the facts of one scene not being such as to lead expectation to the next. This adjective (*epeisodiodes*) is not a particularly happy coinage, but with explanation it is intelligible. And he observes, quite justly, that to be 'epeisodic,' broken into, or

interrupted by, irrelevant scenes, is the worst fault that a play, a tragedy, can have. 'Of all plots and actions the epeisodic are the worst. I call a plot " epeisodic " in which the episodes, or acts, succeed one another without probable or necessary sequence' (*Poet.* IX 10). He adds an interesting remark, that poets, skilful enough to avoid this fault, are sometimes led into it by a desire to accommodate individual actors.

Finally, we may note that Aristotle does not bring these topics (time, place, relevance) into any connexion with one another.

4

Remarks on the Athenian practice and Aristotle's comment

First let me make clear what is *not* found either in Athenian practice or in Aristotle's comments :—

(1) The word 'unity' is never used in regard to the first two topics, limitation of time, and identity of place. Aristotle has no word covering ' Unity' as used in the Renaissance theory of drama ; he has indeed no occasion for any such word.

(2) Neither the practice, or practices, of the dramatists, nor the remarks of Aristotle have anything to do with the ' imitation of Nature,' still less with a delusive resemblance to actual transactions, such that the spectator might fancy himself to be at the place and time of the story. The fact that all the scenes of (say) Euripides' *Hippolytus* are supposed,

and can easily be supposed, to occur within a day, has not the least bearing on the question whether, how far, and in what sense, that play exhibits an imitation of reality. An interval of three days between the curse of Theseus and its fulfilment would make no difference in this respect. Again, the *Ajax* of Sophocles is not less easily conceived as a real occurrence because the action is at one point removed from the tent of Ajax to the shore. Relevance of scenes, upon which Aristotle insists, does not help the *delusion* of reality, but quite the contrary. The insertion of irrelevant scenes would make that conception easier. And in fact neither the tragic poets nor Aristotle show any desire for such a delusion. The Greek plays, with their Chorus and their versified dialogue, are totally unlike reality. Nor did the Greeks feel, so far as we know, that this was an objection. Delusion never occurred to them as an aim ; right or wrong, they did not think of it.

(3) It is not suggested, either by ancient practice or by Aristotle, that the scenes of a drama should be, or conveniently can be, *continuous* in supposed time one with another. The scenes are separated by imaginary gaps of time, conventionally represented by choric songs. Limitation of time, identity of place, relevance of scenes, do not affect this *discontinuity*, which the poets use and which Aristotle assumes as a matter of course.

5

Renaissance critics on Ancient Drama

Now, with this in mind, let us consider the follow
ing. Dryden writes, in the *Essay of Dramatic Poesy*:
(Prof. Ker's Edition, vol. 1, p. 48 f.) :—

> Euripides, in tying himself to one day, has committed an
> absurdity never to be forgiven him; for in one of his tragedies
> [*The Suppliants*, to which reference has been made above] he
> has made Theseus go from Athens to Thebes, which was
> about forty English miles, under the walls of it to give battle,
> and appear victorious in the next act; and yet, from the
> time of his departure to the return of the Nuntius, who
> gives the relation of his victory, Aethra and the Chorus have
> but thirty-six verses; that is not for every mile a verse.

Passages like this are common in the Renaissance
discussions of drama. But Dryden's graceful prose
is extravagant nonsense. For, consider: 'Euripides,'
he says, 'in tying himself to one day...' but *The
Suppliants* is *not* limited to a day ; for it contains, as
appears by Dryden's own reference, a gap in the
action of (say) ten days, and that we are to suppose
these ten days comprised in a day is nowhere at all
suggested.

Again : Thirty-six verses, not a verse to a
mile.... Here is more extravagant nonsense. The
thirty-six verses form a choric song or ode, doubtless accompanied by the usual figures, varied movements fitted to music. Greek Tragedies assume, as
everyone who understood them must see, that such
performances, being *suspensions* of dramatic action,

interludes in fact, are to be used, and are accepted, as equivalents for our drop-scene or curtain. The length of the song, the time taken to perform it, has no more to do with the time supposed to be covered, than has the time taken in lowering and raising the curtain (one minute), which may represent any time required, five minutes, an hour, a day, a week, or whatever the relation of the scenes suggests and requires. If Euripides is here absurd, all Greek tragedies are absurd, for all exhibit choric odes covering by imaginative convention a period of time largely, and often enormously, exceeding the time of performance; such as a battle (in the *Septem* of Aeschylus), a debate in an assembly (Euripides' *Orestes*), the going and return of some person to a place six miles off (Euripides' *Bacchae*), twenty miles off (Sophocles' *Trachiniae*), and so on. In all such cases the 'absurdity' supposed by Dryden's speaker (Charles, Lord Buckhurst, afterwards Lord Dorset, called in the *Essay* Eugenius), is as manifestly present as in the particular case which he has before him. In reality there is no 'absurdity' or 'difficulty' whatever.

Or take this passage from the *Defence of an Essay of Dramatic Poesy* (Prof. Ker's Edition, vol. 1, p. 128) :—

> There is a greater vicinity in nature betwixt two rooms than betwixt two houses; betwixt two houses, than betwixt two cities; and so of the rest: Reason therefore can sooner be led by imagination to step from one room into another, than to walk to [i.e. between] two distant houses, and yet

rather to go thither, than to fly like a witch through the air, and be hurried from one region to another....So then, the less change of place there is, the less time is taken up in transporting the persons of the drama, with analogy to reason; and in that analogy, or *resemblance of fiction to truth*[1], consists the excellency of the play.

And this is supposed to be in some way commended by Aristotle and by the practice of the Ancients!

Again, I can only say that it is extravagant nonsense and has nothing to do with the Ancients; Dryden asserts that, if we as audience are asked to imagine a change in the supposed place of action, we do it more easily if the new place is *near* the other—that it is easier to transfer the scene in imagination from the Great Court of Trinity College to the Nevile than from Trinity to Pembroke, and from Trinity to Pembroke than from Cambridge to London. Everybody who has seen plays, or read stories, and will consider his experience, must know that this is simply false. Yet similar things occur everywhere in the Renaissance controversy.

If Dryden's argument has any substance, how could the scene of the play ever be supposed distant from the place of its performance? Dryden chooses to apply his principle to *change* of scene. But what of the original supposition, at the opening of the play? The curtain goes up, an actor comes on, and we, sitting at the Cambridge Theatre, are told that the place of action is King's Parade, London, Paris, New York, or the Antarctic Circle. Would Dryden,

---

[1] The italics are the lecturer's.

or anybody in his senses, say that our ease in making this supposition instantaneously is proportioned to the real distances, or in the least affected by them ? But why not, if Dryden's principle is sound at all ?

6

How did this nonsense come to be talked by men of sense ?

No one, by natural unprejudiced thinking, could have evolved it. It comes of trying to make a theory of drama which will fit *authorities misunderstood*. The process is common, and this is an instructive example.

The fundamental error consists in a misunderstanding both of the nature of dramatic or other artistic representation and of Aristotle's theory of dramatic representation. Evidently serious drama demands, in some sense, 'imitation of nature.' Macbeth and Othello interest and please us partly because their language and acts seem natural in the circumstances. Even bold imagination owes some respect to nature, if we are to be seriously interested ; there is a 'nature' for dragons : a dragon reasonably 'swinges the scaly horror of his folded tail'; a dragon should not hang out the wash upon drying lines.

And on 'imitation' (*mimesis*) Aristotle insists. His definition of tragedy begins with the words : 'Tragedy is the imitation of an action that is serious, complete,' etc. (*Poetics* VI 2), and he repeats the

phrase more than once (VI 5, 9, VII 2). What he
meant by this, and in particular by the word 'imitation,' is a very abstruse question.   Readers interested
are referred to the discussion in the second chapter
of Professor Butcher's *Aristotle's Theory of Poetry
and Fine Art* (pp. 121–162).   Here I need only say
that Aristotle does make prominent as an element in
tragedy something which he calls 'imitation.'

The error into which the Renaissance critics are
drawn is this: Dramatic imitation means the production in the spectator of a fancy, or a voluntary
delusion that he is bodily present at the place and
time of the supposed action ; and this is what
Aristotle means when he demands 'imitation.'   It
would be easy to show how profound is the error
about Aristotle, but here I must be content to say
that the Greek method of performance excluded all
possibility of delusion.   Yet a consideration of the
passage just quoted from the *Defence of an Essay of
Dramatic Poesy* to which I would recall attention,
evidently assumes that *delusion* is the object.   Such
a view is palpably false, and only confusion and
nonsense could come of it.   The theatre no more
produces delusion than a picture does.

Let us follow out the matter and see what are
the legitimate deductions from the 'delusion' theory:

Deduction 1.   The supposed time of a play should
be equal to the *time required for the performance*.

Observe that here first comes into view the time
of performance—not in the ancient practice, nor in
Aristotle.

Deduction 2. The performance, the supposed action, and the supposed time, should be all *continuous, unbroken*, consisting of one scene, a dialogue, or a series of dialogues naturally leading into one another; there should be no curtain, no drop-scene, no empty stage, nor any equivalent such as the ancient choric odes.

Observe again that here, and not in ancient practice, nor in Aristotle, appears the notion of 'continuity of time.'

Deduction 3. The place, of course, must be identical throughout.

This theory was never perhaps explicitly stated and has certainly never been completely realised; the two first requirements are indeed practically impossible. But it was a legitimate result of the 'delusion' theory, and lurks perpetually behind the Renaissance debate on 'the Unities.'

The resulting problem for the Renaissance critics, then, was: to find these precepts, or something as like them as possible, in the ancient practice and in Aristotle, and their solution of the problem was as follows:

Prescription 1. The ancient 'day' was supposed to be an approximation to the time of performance. Such a supposition is perfectly baseless, and on the face of it false and absurd.

Here is a specimen of the resulting nonsense: Dryden in the *Defence* (Prof. Ker's Edition, vol. 1, p. 129) writes:—

Now, no man ever could suppose, that twenty-four real

> hours could be included in the space of three; but where is
> the absurdity of affirming, that the feigned business of twenty-
> four imagined hours may not more naturally be represented
> in the compass of three real hours, than the like feigned
> business of twenty-four years in the same proportion of real
> time? For the proportions are always real, and much
> nearer,...of twenty-four to three than of four thousand
> to it.

This, of course, is all nonsense. If the 'feigned business' were to be really copied and shown—a thing which Dryden tacitly assumes—'twenty-four hours' could no more be represented in three hours than twenty-four years. Three hours' business and no more could be shown. But in fact no dramatist or audience, ancient or modern, ever thought of showing or seeing the whole business of the time supposed. The business of twenty-four hours is never represented, and in plays where the limit of a day' is most strictly observed the omissions are just as palpable as in the business of a week. *Select pieces*, such as are important and relevant, are shown, and the gaps between these pieces are figured by a curtain or its equivalent (choric ode, etc.), and passed over by the imagination of the audience. This is equally true of Euripides and of Shakespeare. But, this once seen, the notion that the supposed time is *compressed* into the time of performance— twenty-four hours crowded into three, as Dryden says—either by Euripides or by Shakespeare is untenable, and twenty-four years is, so far as concerns the working of the imagination, just as manageable as twenty-four hours. This is not to say that there may not remain reasons for preferring a shorter time, but the desire to come nearer the time of performance is simply irrelevant.

Prescription 2. The performance and the supposed time should be continuous.

The performance in the case of Sophocles and Euripides is in one sense continuous—that is to say, the stage is generally not empty from the beginning to the end. But parts of this performance (choric ode, etc.), are equivalent to curtains, and mark breaks in the supposed time. By ignoring this and confusing continuity of performance with continuity of supposed time, ancient practice in Athenian tragedy and this second prescription might seem to accord. But such a view depends upon the failure to discriminate between scene-dialogue and Chorus.

Further, in Comedy (Plautus and Terence), care was generally taken to make the dialogue continuous *between curtain and curtain*, inside the Acts, so as to avoid an empty stage. The tragedians did the same between ode and ode. This continuity of an Act, which is commendable, is not the same thing as the continuity of the *play*. The plays were not continuous, whether Tragedies or Comedies. But this distinction again could be ignored, and *liaison des scènes* (continuity of the Act) talked about as if it had some bearing on the limitation of the whole time. It is so in Dryden.

Prescription 3. The place should be identical throughout.

This should have been simple, since Euripides

and Sophocles do generally observe this rule, though not on grounds of theory.   But here came in a new element of confusion, a needless debate about the best form of scenery.   Mystery plays required scenes shown in a row side by side, and *in France* the theatre for a time followed suit, as is pointed out by Professor Ker (*Introd.* p. xlv).   The theatre therefore has to show together and all the time places enough for all the scenes of the play—as, for instance, a palace hall and the ground outside of it.   Assuming this, it was of course desirable that the places so combined in stage representation should be places as near as possible together; it would not be satisfactory to have half the stage London and the other half Paris.   Now the 'delusion' theory required that there should be only one scene, and a confused attempt was made to accommodate the requirements of the French theatre to the 'delusion' theory by the audacious assertion, already cited, that the imagination could travel more easily over a short distance than a long one.   The English theatre was never thus embarrassed; there the different scenes were successive, and not simultaneously exhibited or indicated, but the English discussion was affected by the French practice, as we see in Dryden's comments.

Here is a specimen of the resultant nonsense. Dryden writes in the *Defence* (Prof. Ker's Edition, vol. I, p. 128) :—

> For what else concerns the Unity of Place, I have already given my opinion of it in my *Essay*, that there is a latitude

to be allowed to it, as several places in the same town or city, or places adjacent to each other in the same country; *which may all be comprehended under the larger denomination of one place*[1]; yet with this restriction, that the nearer and fewer those imaginary places are, the greater resemblance they will have to truth; and reason, which cannot make them one, will be more easily led to suppose them so.

Here there is visible confusion, explicable only by a knowledge of the preceding history of the various ideas, thus: 'one place' comes from ancient general practice, and the 'delusion' theory; 'nearer' imaginary places from French scenery; 'fewer' imaginary places from the 'delusion' theory qualified in practice; 'greater resemblance to truth' and 'reason more easily led' from the 'delusion' theory supported by false psychology.

7

The word 'Unity'

The word 'Unity,' first applied, I think, to Unity of Action, by which is meant the relevance of all scenes and so the exclusion of unconnected plots— was sharpened to mean the exclusion of any secondary plot whatever. It should be noted that the 'delusion' theory did not theoretically command 'unity of action,' for real proceedings do not exhibit such unity. Yet practically, in a way it did; since the narrowness of the supposed time squeezed out all secondary matter and made one plot, and a thin plot, necessary. Moreover the artistic instinct of

[1] The italics are the lecturer's.

dramatists favoured this 'Unity,' and Aristotle was ready to help.

The combination of stories is the chief excellence of *narrative*; look, for instance, at the multiplicity of plots interwoven in *Tom Jones* or, still more, in *Middlemarch*. If such combination is to be excluded from drama, it is purely by necessity and for theatrical convenience. There is no principle involved; if the plots are all relevant to one another, the principle is satisfied.

The fact that the phrase 'Unity of Action' is also applied to continuity within the Act, the *liaison des scènes*, has introduced a gratuitous element of confusion. And the word 'Unity' was subsequently extended from 'Unity of Action' to include limitation and continuity of time—'Unity of Time'—and identity of place—'Unity of Place.' There is no merit in either application. But the use of the word 'Unity' linked up the whole imbroglio under the name of 'The Three Unities.'

The general question of what should be the length of the action covered by a play, and how far change of scene should be permitted, can of course be separated from the fictions and fallacies of Renaissance critics, but whether with much result seems to me doubtful. On both sides brilliant examples can be cited, and neither Racine's *Andromaque* on the one hand, nor *Macbeth* or *The Winter's Tale*—an extreme case—on the other, must be excluded by any critic's rule. Different effects naturally are produced by the different methods: the effect of

Andromaque depends on the contraction of the story and the close cohesion of the scenes; that of *Macbeth* on diffusion and separation. But such considerations open up a large question, and in any case free discussion is not relevant to Dryden's two Essays, for his whole treatment is entangled in a historical imbroglio and, apart from style, mainly interesting for that reason.

Dryden is readable even when he talks nonsense: and this, of himself, he seldom would do. His entanglement in the errors of his time is noticeable only that we may discount it and do him justice.

8

Other points in Dryden's Essays

But I must not leave the subject of these two Essays without a brief notice of other points of interest to students, besides the treatment of the Unities. One of these, the use of rhyme in plays, was of considerable temporary importance. On this question Dryden changed his mind and his practice. The *Essay of Dramatic Poesy* and the *Defence* belong to the period when he favoured rhyme. Aristotle in his definition of tragedy (*Poet.* VI 2, 3) treats verse both in the scenic dialogue and in the choric odes as a 'seasoning flavouring,' like the ornamental language, and on this principle he might have allowed that rhyme should be given to audiences who by traditional preparation of their ear, or from the nature of their language, required it. Can the matter be

carried much deeper ?   If rhyme is not necessary to
the ear it is certainly inadmissible, since it embarras-
ses the free development and shaping of sentences,
so important to dramatic movement.   Dryden vainly
endeavours to show or to suggest that rhymed verse,
by overlapping, by the arbitrary admission of half
lines, or other devices, can acquire the desirable
freedom.   Later on, led among other reasons by his
admiration for Shakespeare, he came round to the
other side.   But this proves nothing, except for
English, and conceivably not even so much.   We
cannot tell how a new genius might manage to com-
bine the 'freedom' and the 'flavouring.'   Tradition,
however, is adverse and this is an important point.
On the question of Dryden's personal feeling, Professor Ker remarks truly (*Introd*. pp. l, li) that
what Dryden really desired was the rhyme for itself
rather than the rhymed play.   He satisfied his
instinct not in drama at all but in *Absalom and
Achitophel, Palamon and Arcite*, and other such
works.

Many interesting remarks are scattered through
the Essays.   Take for instance the following para-
graph from the *Defence* :—

> But I will be bolder, and do not doubt to make it good,
> though a paradox, that one great reason why prose is not
> to be used in serious plays, is, because it is too near the
> nature of converse: there may be too great a likeness; as the
> most skilful painters affirm, that there may be too near a
> resemblance in a picture: to take every lineament and
> feature is not to make an excellent piece, but to take so
> much only as will make a beautiful resemblance of the whole:

and, with an ingenious flattery of nature, to heighten the beauties of some parts, and hide the deformities of the rest.

Dryden here seems about to shake off the 'delusion' theory altogether. You can have, he says, only such imitation as is compatible with your art-form. This is an approach to the real Aristotle, but it is only a glimpse.

Elsewhere in the *Essay* he tells us that a serious play is Nature wrought up to a higher pitch; 'a play to be like Nature is to be set above it'! And he justifies the decoration of rhyme, like other forms of decoration in the imitative arts, as being an equivalent for the greatness of Nature which is excluded from representation by the scale and conditions necessary to Art.

Earlier in the *Essay* he defends the mixture of tragedy and comedy as not bad in itself if compatible with unity of action :—

And this leads me to wonder why Lisideius and many others should cry up the barrenness of the French plots, above the variety and copiousness of the English. Their plots are single; they carry on one design, which is pushed forward by all the actors, every scene in the play contributing and moving towards it. Our plays, besides the main design, have underplots or by-concernments, of less considerable persons and intrigues, which are carried on with the motion of the main plot: just as they say the orb of the fixed stars and those of the planets, though they have motions of their own, are whirled about by the motion of the *Primum Mobile*, in which they are contained. That similitude expresses much of the English stage; for if contrary motions may be found in nature to agree; if a planet can go east and west at the same time, one way by virtue of his own motion, the other by the force of the First Mover, it will not be difficult to imagine how the under-plot, which is only different, not contrary to the great design, may naturally be conducted along with it.

Yet he confuses himself with the strange and barbarous notion of 'comic *relief*' and says, shortly before :—

> A continued gravity keeps the spirit too much bent ; we must refresh it sometimes, as we bait in a journey, that we may go on with greater ease. A scene of mirth, mixed with tragedy, has the same effect upon us which our music has betwixt the acts; and that we find a relief to us from the best plots and language of the stage, if the discourses have been long. I must therefore have stronger arguments, ere I am convinced that compassion and mirth in the same subject destroy each other.

And here he enters no *caveat* as to unity of action. This view was perhaps impressed upon him by the demands of his audience. In the Preface to *Don Sebastian* he writes: 'I have observed, that the English will not bear a thorough tragedy ; but are pleased, that it should be lightened with under-parts of mirth.'

Both the passages just quoted from the *Essay* are very well written and good specimens of his prose style, and the dignified humour of the comparison of the English stage to the movement of the planets is characteristic.

In a passage, assigned to Lisideius, on dying on the stage there is an excellent touch in the ' Roman gladiator ' :—

I have observed that in all our tragedies, the audience cannot forbear laughing when the actors are to die; it is the most comic part of the whole play. All *passions* may be lively represented on the stage, if to the well-writing of them the actor supplies a good commanded voice, and limbs that move easily, and without stiffness: but there are many *actions* which can never be imitated to a just height: dying especially is a thing which none but a Roman gladiator could naturally perform on the stage, when he did not imitate or represent, but naturally do it; and therefore it is better to omit the representation of it.

In defiance alike of contemporary and Elizabethan practice, he pleads for the abolition of armies on the stage and the substitution of narratives— what he calls 'relations':—

But there is another sort of relations, that is, of things happening in the action of the play, and supposed to be done behind the scenes; and this is many times both convenient and beautiful; for by it the French avoid the tumult which we are subject to in England, by representing duels, battles, and the like; which renders our stage too like the theatres where they fight prizes. For what is more ridiculous than to represent an army with a drum and five men behind it; all which the hero of the other side is to drive in before him; or to see a duel fought, and one slain with two or three thrusts of the foils, which we know are so blunted, that we might give a man an hour to kill another in good earnest with them.

There is good sense here and so also in the replicant, Neander (representing Dryden himself), and his defence of tumultuary scenes, because the English will have them: that is to say, the practical theatre cannot be bound by pure theory; traditional expectation and the 'stream of the people's inclination' must be considered. The artist must be content to do what he should so far as he can.

I must not conclude without drawing attention to the admirable introduction to the *Essay of Dramatic Poesy*, the raising of interest by the allusion to the battle of June 3, 1665 : 'It was that memorable day, in the first summer of the late war, when our navy engaged the Dutch'; and the skilful passage to the critical discussion of toleration : 'Crites...said, smiling to us, that if the concernment of this battle had not been so exceeding great, he could scarce have wished the victory at the price he knew he must pay for it, in being subject to the reading and hearing of so many ill verses as he was sure would be made upon it.'

VI

THE RELIGIOUS POEMS

Religio Laici and *The Hind and the Panther*

For Dryden's religious opinions there is little evidence until we come to his two religious poems published respectively in November 1682 and April 1687. Nor is there any reason why there should be such evidence. In 1686 we have the startling circumstances of his public conversion at a time of national crisis, conversion to the views of the King but to the unpopular side. His motives are perhaps ambiguous, but he has always stood for the representative renegade. The biographical problem is interesting to men of letters, whether they like or dislike Dryden, and has been discussed, among others, by Johnson, Scott, Macaulay, and Mr Saintsbury.

As to the times before 1681 there is little to say. Dryden was not a public man, and did not directly discuss political or religious subjects. He was a professed member of the Church of England and a 'King's servant'; a 'prerogative man' in politics, when he thought of it, and a royalist, though not of the Anglican religious type, the type devoted to the 'blessed memory' of 'Charles the Martyr.' Dryden's type was rather that of the royalist of the Long Parliament, before the acute division of parties; he was a Churchman by profession, and thought the profession of Churchmanship sufficient. For his general views, besides the tone of *Religio Laici* and the statements in *The Hind and the Panther* (to be quoted later) there is evidence in the Preface to *Tyrannic Love* (printed 1670) and in the *State of Innocence*[1] (1674). No piety is shown in either, and the general attitude suggested is one of scepticism.

Dryden's private conduct is not strictly relevant to the question of his religious opinions and I shall not here discuss it, beyond briefly saying that there is nothing to show that he fell below his profession, according to the standard of the day. Again his literary offences are not relevant to his creed, though they disprove the maintenance of a severe standard; that, however, he did not profess to maintain. Burnet's[2] description of him as 'a monster of impurity' is mere rhetoric, and any inference therefrom as to Dryden's religious belief is wholly inadmissible.

What is clear is that he had a marked dislike of clergy of all sorts, as such. Was this due to his own impatience of restriction? Or to unreasonable demands on the part of the clergy? There is perhaps something of both in his attitude, but neither is the main point. The main point is that he

---

[1] See below, p. 217.   [2] See above, p. 25.

regarded the clergy in general as tiresome disturbers
of peace: his feeling is represented, for instance,
in the character of the Mufti in *Don Sebastian*
(published in 1690) in speaking of whom Benducar
says :—

> For churchmen, though they itch to govern all,
> Are silly, woeful, awkward politicians :
> They make lame mischief, though they mean it well.

The view was common among laymen at that time,
and not unnatural to men who remembered the
Bishops' War, or the conduct of Laud on the one
hand, and of the Puritans on the other. To many
laymen a 'clergyman' seemed only half a 'King's
subject.' Dryden constantly derides the pretensions
of the clergy to high character : see his Spanish
Friar (1681–2) as well as the Mufti. In considering
his views about religion we must alike disregard both
his prejudice against the clergy, and clerical insinua-
tions, such as those of Burnet, against him.

Real Christianity was not fashionable at this
time and Deism was regarded as the 'Natural
Religion.' The main points of Deism are noted in
Religio Laici (42–61): God is worshipped by praise
and prayer, and by repentance; there is a com-
pensatory future state ; evidence for the existence of
this the Deists professed to derive from 'Reason':—

> Our Reason prompts us to a future state,
> The last appeal from Fortune and from Fate,
> When God's all-righteous ways will be declar'd,
> The bad meet punishment, the good reward.

Dryden in *The Hind and the Panther* (published

in April, 1687) admits that he has held no recognised creed :—

> My pride struck out new sparkles of her own.   (1 75)

His creed was presumably some sort of Deism. Mr Firth's note[1] on this passage from *The Hind and the Panther* (1 62–78) attaches 'great autobiographical importance' to these lines, which 'help to explain Dryden's conversion to Roman Catholicism.' This view is confirmed by the incidental evidence of Dryden's earlier works. *The State of Innocence* is really Deistic and not Christian in tone ; in his play of *Tyrannic Love*, the religion of St Catharine may be mere philosophy.   In the Preface to that play he disclaims profanity, writing as follows : ' I am charged by some ignorant or malicious persons with no less crimes than profaneness and irreligion.' Then after defending his treatment of Maximin, which had been attacked by his critics, he concludes : ' This, reader, is what I owed to my just defence, and the due reverence of that religion which I profess, to which all men, who desire to be esteemed good, or honest, are obliged....I ask leave to add ' (in further evidence besides the witness of his ' own conscience, which abhors the thought of such a crime') 'my outward conversation, which shall never be justly taxed with the note of atheism or profaneness.'   But this disclaimer proves nothing as to his positive belief ; Deism is not profane.

[1] In his revision of Christie's Edition of *Select Poems by Dryden* (Clarendon Press, 1901).

Then we come to the political crisis of 1680, purely political as presented by Dryden (in *Absalom and Achitophel*), but at root religious, and likely to stimulate in Dryden interest in theology. Dryden's party, the National party, was largely composed of real Anglicans, and very important services were rendered to the party by the Anglican clergy, especially the rural clergy. The City, the centre of the opposite party, was largely Presbyterian and sectarian, representing Dryden's heartily disliked 'private interpretation,' combined with Republicanism. Further, Dryden was now passing out of middle life; he was fifty years of age, and a deeper consideration of the problems of theology was quite natural, even without external impulse.

Close consideration of *Absalom and Achitophel* shows that Dryden's position was, even at that date (November, 1681), very dubiously Anglican. He emphasises, as we saw[1], the 'native right' of the Roman Catholics, 'Jebusites,' as they are there called (85 ff.), and his coarse satire on Transubstantiation (118 ff.) shows rather religious insensibility than hostile theology. Again the poem shows his dislike of liberty and private judgement :—

> Gods they had tried of every shape and size
> That godsmiths could produce or priests devise. (49 f.)

His subsequent approach to religion is avowedly political, as is shown in the Preface to *Religio Laici* by his manner of dealing both with 'Papists' and with 'Sectarians.'

[1] See above, p. 83.

This Preface is very well written. Its whole professed purpose is to find a religious settlement which will support the English monarchical and limited constitution. He has no difficulty in showing, by an appeal to history, that if *one* system is to be universal it must be the Anglican; neither Roman Catholicism nor Free Churches can be universally acceptable in England. His demand of proof for the truth of revealed religion is very easy; 'Let us be content at last to know God by his own methods; at least, so much of him as he is pleased to reveal to us in the sacred Scriptures: to apprehend them to be the word of God is all our reason has to do; for all beyond it is the work of faith, which is the seal of Heaven impressed upon our human understanding.' On the question of 'faith' in the Popish Plot, the Preface contains a cutting hit at 'Fanatics': 'As for the late design, Mr Coleman's letters, for aught I know, are the best evidence; and what they discover, without wire-drawing their sense or malicious glosses, all men of reason conclude credible. If there be anything more than this required of me, I must believe it as well as I am able, in spite of the witnesses, and out of a decent conformity to the votes of Parliament; for I suppose the Fanatics will not allow the private spirit in this case.'

Religio Laici is an exposition of Anglicanism: Deism will not do; Heaven must be revealed. Christianity is taken on its moral merits: but what of those who have not heard its truths? Their

salvation must be possible : ' It has always been my
thought, that heathens who never did, nor without
miracle could, hear of the name of Christ, were yet
in a possibility of salvation.' So he writes in the
Preface, and in the poem itself his view is thus
expressed :—

> Then, those who follow'd Reason's dictates right,
> Liv'd up, and lifted high their natural light,
> With Socrates may see their Maker's face,
> While thousand rubric-martyrs want a place.
>
> (208 ff.)

This brings him to the consideration of the Athan-
asian Creed :—

> Nor does it baulk my charity to find
> The Egyptian Bishop of another mind,

and to the expression of the view that even for
Christians not much theology is desirable. Raising
this vital point, Dryden adds :—

> Shall I speak plain, and in a nation free
> Assume an honest layman's liberty ?
> I think, according to my little skill,
> To my own mother Church submitting still,
> That many have been sav'd, and many may,
> Who never heard this question brought in play.
> The unletter'd Christian, who believes in gross,
> Plods on to Heaven and ne'er is at a loss ;
> For the strait gate would be made straiter yet,
> Were none admitted there but men of wit.
>
> (316 ff.)

But what guarantee is there for Revelation ?
Dryden, as a scholar, admits that the Book of the
Scriptures rests on tradition. In doubt, where then

is authority? This question is vaguely handled by him and his conclusion is practically based upon English politics. Papist and Protestant ' Fanatics ' are alike rejected, and a vague assumption is made that in what is needful the Scriptures are clear :—

> 'Tis some relief, that points not clearly known
> Without much hazard may be let alone;

and then he comes to the *practical* point :—

> And after hearing what our Church can say,
> If still our reason runs another way,
> That private reason 'tis more just to curb
> Than by disputes the public peace disturb.
> For points obscure are of small use to learn :
> But common quiet is mankind's concern.   (443 ff.)

The style is admirable in its ease and flexibility. A striking passage expresses the plain man's disgust at fictitious demands upon ignorance, and his dislike of priestcraft ; in his account of the medieval clergy, Dryden recalls Chaucer ; like Chaucer he brings out the humour of the thing :—

> In times o'ergrown with rust and ignorance
> A gainful trade their clergy did advance ;
> When want of learning kept the laymen low
> And none but priests were authoriz'd to know ;
> When what small knowledge was in them did dwell
> And he a God who could but read or spell ;
> Then Mother Church did mightily prevail ;
> She parcell'd out the Bible by retail,
> But still expounded what she sold or gave,
> To keep it in her power to damn and save.
> Scripture was scarce, and as the market went,
> Poor laymen took salvation on content,

As needy men take money, good or bad ;
God's word they had not, but the priest's they had.
Yet, whate'er false conveyances they made,
The lawyer still was certain to be paid.
In those dark times they learn'd their knack so well,
That by long use they grew infallible.
At last, a knowing age began to inquire
If they the Book or that did them inspire ;
And making narrower search they found, though late,
That what they thought the priest's was their estate,
Taught by the will produc'd, the written word,
How long they had been cheated on record.
Then every man, who saw the title fair,
Claim'd a child's part and put in for a share,
Consulted soberly his private good,
And sav'd himself as cheap as e'er he could.   (370 ff.)

Dryden had too much wit to pose as a prophet but was not ill-pleased to find himself on a platform. The ostensible occasion for the poem—a friend's translation of a book on criticism of the Old Testament—is a mere pretext, but serves well.

Now in all this, is there any religion at all? *Religio Laici* might well be dismissed as mere politics but for its astounding commencement. That this is a mere assumption for a political purpose, I cannot admit; after reading the Preface, the opening of the poem surprises me fresh every time :—

Dim as the borrow'd beams of moon and stars
To lonely, weary, wandering travellers
Is Reason to the soul: and as on high
Those rolling fires discover but the sky,
Not light us here, so Reason's glimmering ray
Was lent, not to assure our doubtful way,
But guide us upward to a better day.

And as those nightly tapers disappear
When day's bright lord ascends our hemisphere,
So pale grows Reason at Religion's sight,
So dies, and so dissolves in supernatural light.

The Hind and the Panther

We have seen the sandy foundations of *Religio Laici*. Dryden's hatred of ' private judgement,' the difficulty of distinguishing his actual position, his strong language on the desirability of infallible authority :—

Such an omniscient Church we wish indeed;
'Twere worth both Testaments, and cast in the Creed;

—all point to his future conversion. This is noted by several of his critics, and more particularly by Mr Saintsbury, who discusses the question in the fifth chapter of his *Life of Dryden* in the earlier series of *English Men of Letters*, edited by Lord Morley.

Dryden's conversion to Roman Catholicism took place soon after the accession of James II, and is often attributed to that event, and to that event alone. But Dryden's interest in the change is not so clear as his adverse critics would have us suppose. Before his conversion James had confirmed his tenure of the posts of Poet Laureate and Historiographer Royal, and the salary pertaining to those posts was more likely to be regularly paid under the administration of James than it had been under that of Charles. The grant, soon after his conversion, of an additional pension of £100 a year was no new thing, but only the renewal of the pension originally granted by Charles. No doubt his comfort at Court was largely increased by his change of religion, and we may say that there was probably an immediate advantage in his conversion. But the advantage was very precarious, depending as it did on the life of James; the life of James, however, was perhaps good enough security for Dryden. It has been said that Dryden 'did not foresee the Revolution'; this is true but not the whole truth; James's policy was good only till the meeting of Parliament, and that at the meeting of Parliament renegades were likely to suffer, Dryden well knew. The 'wary savage,' the Panther, standing for the Church of England, would not give offence to the King:—

> But watched the time her vengeance to complete,
> When all her furry sons in frequent senate met,

and other references in Dryden's writings show his recognition of the danger. Parliament had been prorogued on November 20, 1685, and met no more in the reign of James II. But such a state of things could not have continued indefinitely. On the whole therefore, and considering the internal evidence of the two religious poems, Dryden is entitled to suspense of judgement; we cannot inspect his conscience.

After his conversion in 1686 he was employed by the Government in prose controversy against Stillingfleet, 'the grim logician' of the Third Part of *The Hind and the Panther* (193 ff.). But this was not Dryden's line, and he soon turned to verse.

The first policy of James II had been to induce the Church of England to share her position with the Roman Catholics, and he hoped, with the support of the Anglican party, to obtain the abolition of the Test. When this failed he adopted a new policy, under which all sects, including the Roman Catholics, were to ally together against the Church of England. In accordance with this later policy, he issued the Declaration of Indulgence—bestowed, that is to say, toleration by royal prerogative—in April 1687, shortly before the publication of *The Hind and the Panther.* The inconsistency of the general tone of the poem with the King's newly-declared policy is admitted by Dryden in his Preface. 'There are many of our sects...who have withdrawn themselves from the communion of the Panther and embraced this gracious Indulgence of his Majesty in point of toleration. But...this Satire...is aimed only at the refractory and disobedient on either side. For those who have come over to the royal party are consequently supposed to be out of gun-shot.' And again, 'About a fortnight before I had finished [the poem], his Majesty's Declaration for Liberty of Conscience came abroad : which if I had so soon expected, I might have spared myself the labour of writing many things which are contained in the Third Part of it.'

On this subject of liberty of conscience he here writes as follows : 'I may safely say, that conscience is the royalty and prerogative of every private man. He is absolute in his own breast, and accountable to no earthly power for that which passes only betwixt God and him.' Such strong expressions, whether in the Preface or in the poem, would be more estimable had they preceded the announcement of the King's policy, or had Dryden so spoken generally. But they contrast strikingly with his peremptory treatment of Schismatics of the English Church in the Preface to *Religio Laici*: 'Thus sectaries, we may see, were born with teeth, foul-mouthed and scurrilous from their infancy; and if spiritual pride, venom, violence, contempt of superiors, and slander had been the marks of orthodox belief, the Presbytery and the rest of our Schismatics, which are their spawn, were always the most visible Church in the Christian world.' If, he concludes, they think themselves too roughly handled by him, 'the best way for them to confute' him is 'to disclaim their principles and renounce their practices.' Not much respect here for liberty of conscience!

The motive of the King's policy was suspected and his political method detested: the Declaration of Indulgence was an arbitrary act contrary to the Constitution and threatening danger to the rights of Parliament. This point Dryden never touches. Did he see it? Did he ignore it? Either way, the omission is fatal to any political application of his poem.

We pass from the Preface to the poem itself. The sects are called by various beast-names: the 'milk-white' Hind represents the Roman Catholics, the Wolf stands for the Calvinists, the quaking Hare for the Quakers, and so on. The Hind is protected

by the Lion, representing the King. The Church
of England is typified by the Panther, beautiful but
spotty.

On these lines no story is possible, and none is
attempted. The poem, in three large Books, consists of talk on the situation between the Anglican
and the Roman Catholic. The story is simply that
the Hind, meeting the Panther with other beasts at
their watering-place, invites her to walk home, and
then spend the night at her 'cottage' (ii 675); the
two talk. Even this is absurd. How about supper?
There is nothing for the Panther except the Hind.
Dryden was well aware of the absurdity; the
Panther, we are told,

> civilly drew in her sharpen'd paws,
> Not violating hospitable laws,
> And pacified her tail and lick'd her frothy jaws.
>
> (ii 718 ff.)

and again :—

> Others our Hind of folly will indite
> To entertain a dangerous guest by night.
> Let those remember that she cannot die
> Till rolling time is lost in round eternity. (iii 16 ff.)

Here Dryden plainly winks.

What then is the object of introducing the beast-
names? Merely to divert attack from an amateur
theologian as such, in anticipation of such an attack
upon the poem as was in fact made by Montague
and Prior in *The Country and the City Mouse*.
The 'beasts' are an excuse for lowering the theme
of the poem; there was on this occasion to be none

of the pomp of *Absalom and Achitophel*, where the
Biblical story was employed as a device for height-
ening the theme.

The personal and religious note is struck early
in the poem :—

> But, gracious God, how well dost thou provide
> For erring judgements an unerring guide!
> Thy throne is darkness in the abyss of light,
> A blaze of glory that forbids the sight.
> O teach me to believe Thee thus conceal'd,
> And search no farther than Thyself reveal'd ;
> But her alone for my director take,
> Whom Thou hast promis'd never to forsake!
> My thoughtless youth was wing'd with vain desires ;
> My manhood, long misled by wandering fires,
> Follow'd false lights ; and when their glimpse was gone
> My pride struck out new sparkles of her own.
> Such was I, such by nature still I am ;
> Be Thine the glory, and be mine the shame! (1 64 ff.)

There is nothing like this in *Religio Laici* ; are we
to say that it is hypocrisy ?

The notion of a bargain for salvation is still
pursued, as in the earlier poem, but Dryden now
will have a guarantee, and reprobates the peddling
of *Religio Laici* :—

> To take up half on trust and half to try,
> Name it not faith, but bungling bigotry.
> Both knave and fool the merchant we may call
> To pay great sums and to compound the small,
> For who would break with Heaven, and would not break
>   for all ?   (1 141 ff.)

Then we come to the Calvinist Wolf :—

> More haughty than the rest, the wolfish race
> Appear with belly gaunt and famish'd face ;
> Never was so deform'd a beast of grace.
> His ragged tail betwixt his legs he wears,
> Close clapp'd for shame ; but his rough crest he rears,
> And pricks up his predestinating ears.   (1 160 ff.)

This description is followed by the famous denunciation of Geneva, the home of Calvin—Geneva, situated on the shores of Lake Leman and close under the Jura and the mountains of Savoy :—

> What though your native kennel still be small,
> Bounded betwixt a puddle and a wall ;
> Yet your victorious colonies are sent
> Where the North Ocean girds the continent.
> Quicken'd with fire below, your monsters breed
> In fenny Holland and in fruitful Tweed ;   209
> And, like the first, the last affects to be
> Drawn to the dregs of a democracy.   (1 204 ff.)

In *v.* 209 I suggest that the reading should be not 'in fruitful' (two words) but 'infruitful'; a derogatory epithet is wanted to pair with 'fenny' Holland, and the barrenness of Scotland was, as we know, a stock commonplace of the time and the subject of more than one allusion[1] in *Absalom and Achitophel*.

After an indiscreet admission (291 ff.) that Italy and Spain are models for England, Dryden passes to an unworthy denunciation of the rural sects :—

> A slimy-born and sun-begotten tribe,
> Who, far from steeples and their sacred sound,
> In fields their sullen conventicles found.   (1 311 ff.)

[1] See above, p. 75.

The haughtiness is offensive, and we must not forget that the sects did not choose their solitude, but were driven into it. But the expression is admirably vigorous :—

> Souls that can scarce ferment their mass of clay,
> So drossy, so divisible are they
> As would but serve pure bodies for allay. (I 318 ff.)

The mixed character of the Panther, the Church of England, is utilised as one would expect. Dryden draws attention to the local character of the institution :—

> To foreign lands no sound of her is come,
> Humbly content to be despised at home; (I 404 f.)

to the absence of authority to control private judgement :—

> As long as words a different sense will bear,
> And each may be his own interpreter,
> Our airy faith will no foundation find;
> The word's a weathercock for every wind. (I 462 ff.)

and passes to the epigrammatic conclusion :—

> O solid rock, on which secure she stands!
> Eternal house, not built with mortal hands!
> O sure defence against the infernal gate,
> A patent during pleasure of the State! (I 493 ff.)

This part of the poem brings out clearly what may be called Dryden's political objection to Anglicanism, namely, that it is no safe foundation for civil authority, for, as 'God's and kings' rebels have the same good cause,' the Anglican Church

> wants innate auctority;
> For how can she constrain them to obey
> Who has herself cast off the lawful sway?

11—2

The same point is made again at some length in
Part II :—

> But soon against your superstitious lawn
> Some Presbyterian sabre would be drawn;
> In your established laws of sovereignty
> The rest some fundamental flaw would see,
> And call rebellion gospel-liberty.   (II 411 ff.)

In the Second Part the Panther, discussing
authority, soon raises the question of infallibility :—

> But, shunning long disputes, I fain would see
> That wondrous wight, Infallibility.
> Is he from Heaven, this mighty champion, come?
> Or lodg'd below in subterranean Rome?
> First, seat him somewhere, and derive his race,
> Or else conclude that nothing has no place. (II 64 ff.)

To this passage Christie oddly appends the following note :—' " Roma Sotteranea," an extensive
cavern near Rome, formerly inhabited, described in
a work of that name published at Rome, circa 1632,'
and does not add that this 'extensive cavern' is
better known as 'the Catacombs.'   The book which
he mentions is A. Bosio's account of his exploration
of 'Subterranean Rome.'

The opening words of the Hind's answer :—

> 'Suppose, (though I disown it,)' said the Hind,
> 'The certain mansion were not yet assign'd :
> The doubtful residence no proof can bring
> Against the plain existence of the thing.
> Because philosophers may disagree
> If sight by emission or reception be,
> Shall it be thence inferr'd I do not see?'   (II 70 ff.)

are thus commented on by Johnson : 'Dryden is weak enough to ask, why, since we see, without knowing how, we may not have an infallible judge without knowing where.' Johnson's criticism, which has met with the approval of others, is plausible but clearly not fair. Dryden takes the authority of the Church as a fact of historical experience, 'the plain existence of the thing' is not in his view disputable.

After an account of Popes and General Councils, etc., and a discussion on the value respectively of Scripture and Tradition—a lively and simple narrative impossible to summarise—we come upon a passage almost tragically impressive :—

> 'If not by Scriptures, how can we be sure,'
> Replied the Panther, 'what tradition's pure?
> For you may palm upon us new for old;
> "All," as they say, "that glitters is not gold."'
> 'How but by following her,' replied the dame,
> 'To whom deriv'd from sire to son they came ;
> Where every age does on another move,
> And trusts no farther than the next above ;
> Where all the rounds like Jacob's ladder rise,
> The lowest hid in earth, the topmost in the skies?'
> Sternly the savage did her answer mark,
> Her glowing eye-balls glittering in the dark,
> And said but this :—'Since lucre was your trade,
> Succeeding times such dreadful gaps have made,
> 'Tis dangerous climbing : to your sons and you
> I leave the ladder, and its omen too.'   (II 212 ff.)

The omen of the gallows! The Panther, in a difficulty, escapes by a political threat, consonant with the tone of the times. Did Dryden feel the horror?

Apparently he did feel it a little, and that, for the age, is much.

The subject is continued at length—Apostles (307), Epistles (335) and so on. The Hind still puts the dilemma, that if Scripture is to be the authority, an expositor is necessary ; if tradition, tradition must be taken entire, as by the Roman Catholics. Dryden's Hind makes real points in this discourse :—

> It then remains, that Church can only be
> The guide which owns unfailing certainty ;   (II 483 f.)
>
> *   *   *   *
>
> But this unfailing universal State
> You shun, nor dare succeed to such a glorious weight ;
>   (II 491 f.)
>
> *   *   *   *
>
> All which the Mother-Church asserts her own,
> And with unrivalled claim ascends the throne.   (II 497 f.)

The essence of Dryden's position is this : he must have a guarantee ; only one dealer offers a guarantee ; let us close, therefore, with this dealer, and then do not haggle over details.

At this point he seems to feel the need for lifting the theme ;—and he lifts it. His comparison of the Church as the only adequate guarantor, to the Redeemer as alone able to discharge man's obligation, suggests the well known Miltonic passage in the Third Book of *Paradise Lost* (56–415), a passage which Dryden compresses, with a gain of strength and tenderness :—

> So, when of old the Almighty Father sate,
> In council to redeem our ruin'd state,

Millions of millions, at a distance round,
Silent the sacred consistory crown'd,
To hear what mercy mix'd with justice could propound;
All prompt with eager pity to fulfil
The full extent of their Creator's will.
But when the stern conditions were declar'd,
A mournful whisper through the host was heard,
And the whole hierarchy with heads hung down
Submissively declin'd the ponderous proffer'd crown.
Then, not till then, the eternal Son from high
Rose in the strength of all the Deity;
Stood forth to accept the terms, and underwent
A weight which all the frame of heaven had bent,
Nor he himself could bear, but as omnipotent. (II 499 ff.)

Then we have a description of the marks of the true Church, and incidentally touch a historical point of some interest in the severe remarks on English missions, or rather on the lack of them (II 556 ff.).

So we arrive at the Hind's cottage. The Hind is poor and the Panther rich. Here Dryden begins to jest. The Hind, for instance, begs the Panther to stay,

For fear she might be wilder'd in her way,
Because she wanted an unerring guide.   (II 682 f.)

In her words of welcome there is a strange mixture of classical allusion and Christian theology :—

This peaceful seat my poverty secures;
War seldom enters but where wealth allures:
Nor yet despise it, for this poor abode
Has oft receiv'd and yet receives a God;
A God victorious of the Stygian race
Here laid his sacred limbs, and sanctified the place.
This mean retreat did mighty Pan contain.   (II 705 ff.)

The point is, I think, that the humblest church contains the Corpus Christi : so the Hind's poor abode contains God.

The Third Part opens with much personal detail of Dryden's controversy with Stillingfleet, and is tedious unless we are filled with the subject. In one place I would suggest a change in punctuation. The Panther, following the line taken by Stillingfleet, is denying that the immediate cause of the separation of Henry VIII from the Church of Rome was the Pope's refusal to grant him a divorce from Catherine of Arragon. The passage runs as follows :—

> Thus, our eighth Henry's marriage they defame ;
> They say the schism of beds began the game,
> Divorcing from the Church to wed the dame ;
> Though largely prov'd, and by himself profess'd,
> That conscience, conscience would not let him rest,
> I mean, not till possess'd of her he lov'd,   208
> And old, uncharming Catherine was remov'd.
> For sundry years before did he complain,
> And told his ghostly confessor his pain !
>
> (III 203 ff.)

As commonly punctuated, *v.* 208 is inconsistent with the view expressed by the Panther, who is supposed to be maintaining the sincerity of Henry's reforming zeal, and controverting the suggestion of a personal motive, whereas, with a comma after 'I mean,' the Panther's case is given away. By placing the comma after 'not,'

> I mean not, till possessed of her he loved...

the consistency of the Panther's tone is kept and there is no break in the irony of the passage.

This part contains the finest passages of the poem. Dryden's sufferings under obloquy were real and severe; the story of his distress 'even with tears,' at the usage he had received in *The Country and the City Mouse*, though probably apocryphal, is representative of his sensitiveness to some kinds of criticism. When the Hind resents on behalf of her sons the imputation of Atheism, and yet will not retort with personal satire, evidently the Hind speaks for Dryden, who did in the main abstain from personal venom. Many professed Anglicans were an easy mark for satire—Burnet, satirised as the Buzzard, had attacked Dryden—but he hits not only his opponents but both sides, in a humorous way. He here professes to disclaim revenge, or even self-defence, on religious grounds, accepting the duties of sacrifice and of humility. Whether this profession on his part is sincere or not, he gets the note in the magnificent passage :—

> Be vengeance wholly left to powers divine,
> And let Heaven judge betwixt your sons and mine :
> If joys hereafter must be purchas'd here
> With loss of all that mortals hold so dear,
> Then welcome infamy and public shame,
> And last, a long farewell to worldly fame.
> 'Tis said with ease, but oh, how hardly tried
> By haughty souls to human honour tied !
> O sharp convulsive pangs of agonizing pride !
> Down then, thou rebel, never more to rise ;
> And what thou did'st and dost so dearly prize,

That fame, that darling fame, make that thy sacrifice.
'Tis nothing thou hast given; then add thy tears
For a long race of unrepenting years :
'Tis nothing yet, yet all thou hast to give :
Then add those may-be years thou hast to live :
Yet nothing still ; then poor and naked come,
Thy Father will receive his unthrift home,
And thy blest Saviour's blood discharge the mighty sum.

(III 279 ff.)

After an interesting passage on the present balance of advantage between Roman Catholicism and Anglicanism, too long to quote, he passes to the episodes.

To these Dryden's Preface, not without reason, calls attention. The Hind and the Panther each tell a moral fable satirising the present policy of the opponent. The Panther relates the tale of the Swallows, who, deceived by fair weather out of season and counting on its continuance, postponed their departure and were destroyed by the prompt return of winter. This is an obvious reference to the sanguine hopes built by some (but not all) Catholics on the forward policy of James. There was a division of opinion on this subject in the Catholic party. The Moderates would have been content to better their position, so far as with the King's help they could do so, within the limits of English law; the Forwards preferred to back the King in his invasion of the Anglican barriers in the existing Constitution, and to defy Parliament. The fable of the Swallows, though of course assigned

to the Anglican speaker, shows that Dryden, *qua*
Catholic, was a Moderate, and already, before the Declaration of Indulgence, had deep mistrust of James.

The principal Forward was Father Petre, the
Jesuit, who 'among the evil counsellors' of James
'bore perhaps the largest part in the ruin of the
House of Stuart[1],' nobly born, ignorant of business, presumptuous, and misunderstanding English
feeling.   Dryden evidently disliked him profoundly.
He figures in the fable as the Martin, the chief
author of the advice by which the swallows are
ruined.   Petre as a public man was a fair object of
criticism ; still probably neither he nor his partisans
were quite satisfied with Dryden's explanation (III
640–646) that the following sketch should be set
down to mere malice in the Panther.   The young
swallows, discouraged by a gale, propose to put off
their migration :—

> With these the Martin readily concurr'd,
> A church-begot and church-believing bird ;
> Of little body, but of lofty mind,
> Round bellied, for a dignity design'd,
> And much a dunce, as Martins are by kind ;
> Yet often quoted Canon-laws and Code
> And Fathers which he never understood ;
> But little learning needs in noble blood.
> For, sooth to say, the Swallow brought him in
> Her household chaplain and her next of kin :
> In superstition silly to excess,
> And casting schemes by planetary guess ;
> In fine, short-wing'd, unfit himself to fly,
> His fear foretold foul weather in the sky. (III 461 ff.)

[1] Macaulay's *History*, Vol. II. Ch. VI.

The story of the Swallows is the best thing in the poem. Of the temporary prosperity of the Court Catholics, the most is made by the Irish among the King's friends—Swifts in the fable. The lively and picturesque prophecy of the catastrophe foreshows the adapter of Chaucer and of Boccaccio, authors with whom the concluding passage of the Preface shows that he was already familiar. The whole passage is too long to quote here ; the first few lines must suffice :—

> What should they do, beset with dangers round,
> No neighbouring dorp, no lodging to be found,
> But bleaky plains, and bare unhospitable ground?
> The latter brood, who just began to fly,
> Sick-feather'd and unpractis'd in the sky,
> For succour to their helpless mother call :
> She spread her wings ; some few beneath them crawl ;
> She spread them wider yet, but could not cover all.
> To augment their woes, the winds began to move
> Debate in air for empty fields above,
> Till Boreas got the skies, and pour'd amain
> His rattling hailstones mix'd with snow and rain.

(III 610 ff.)

Some more politics follow, chiefly about the Anglican Test, and we have some very smart rhetoric from the Anglican on the Roman Catholic notion of a fair division. The situation is compared with the relations of Aeneas and Latinus in the later books of the *Aeneid*. The Catholics, like the Trojan invaders, plead their ancient rights, but anyhow bring their own gods :—

> Methinks such terms of proffer'd peace you bring
> As once Aeneas to the Italian king.

By long possession all the land is mine ;
You strangers come with your intruding line
To share my sceptre, which you call to join.
You plead like him an ancient pedigree
And claim a peaceful seat by Fate's decree :
In ready pomp your sacrificer stands,
To unite the Trojan and the Latin bands .
And, that the league more firmly may be tied,
Demand the fair Lavinia for your bride.
Thus plausibly you veil the intended wrong,
But still you bring your exil'd gods along ;
And will endeavour, in succeeding space,
Those household poppits on our hearths to place.

(III 766 ff.)

Finally, the Panther proving impracticable on the question of the Test, the Hind proposes to relate the story of the Pigeons and their king the Buzzard, satirising the recent move of the High Church Anglicans—the Pigeons—towards the Latitudinarians, the English Churchmen, that is, who were indulgent to Dissenters. This attitude Dryden represents as submission to the typical Latitudinarian, Burnet. The moral of the fable is that the king Buzzard will do after his kind and plunder the Pigeons more effectually than their supposed enemies could do. The fiction is not happy ; the King (the Farmer) keeps both Pigeons (Anglicans) and Poultry (Catholics) and prefers the Poultry. The plain objection is that James did not *eat* Catholics ; yet this is implied in his distaste for Pigeons' meat. The analogy becomes grotesque when Dryden writes of the Pigeons :—

> Their flesh was never to the table serv'd;
> Though tis not thence inferr'd the birds were starv'd;
> But that their master did not like the food,
> As rank, and breeding melancholy blood.   (III 974 ff.)

Nor does the Buzzard as a protector of Pigeons well suit the alliance of the Higher Anglicans with a Latitudinarian and semi-Presbyterian such as Burnet.   In the fable the Buzzard is brought to the dovecote, but at the time when the poem was written Burnet, who was hated by James, was in exile at the Court of the Prince of Orange.   Burnet, who had spoken severely of Dryden, as indeed of most people, is brilliantly described by Macaulay in the second volume (chapter VII) of his *History of England*; briefly, we may say that he was forward, eloquent, indiscreet, honest, and pugnacious. Dryden's satiric portrait (1140 ff.) is good but too long; only the spirited conclusion can be quoted here :—

> Prompt to assail, and careless of defence,
> Invulnerable in his impudence,
> He dares the world and, eager of a name,
> He thrusts about and justles into fame.
> Frontless and satire-proof, he scours the streets,
> And runs an Indian muck at all he meets.
> So fond of loud report, that not to miss
> Of being known (his last and utmost bliss),
> He rather would be known for what he is.
>
> (III 1185 ff.)

The Doves of course repent their invitation and are said to lose credit and to suffer from their Presbyterian director ; the reader may sympathise with the Panther :—

Thus did the gentle Hind her fable end,
Nor would the Panther blame it nor commend ;
But, with affected yawnings, at the close,
Seem'd to require her natural repose.   (III 1289 ff.)

The strange poem ends, as it began, with
Dryden's softest music :—

For now the streaky light began to peep,
And setting stars admonish'd both to sleep.
The dame withdrew, and wishing to her guest
The peace of Heaven, betook herself to rest.
Ten thousand angels on her slumbers wait
With glorious visions of her future state. (III 1293 ff.)

VII

THE DEVELOPMENT OF THE ENGLISH
ODE; DRYDEN'S INFLUENCE ON
LYRIC POETRY

THE word Ode is used in English with a certain
vagueness, often only as an equivalent to Song.
The best known Odes of antiquity, from which is
derived the English use of the name, are those of
Horace and of Pindar, in particular the *Epinikia*,
or triumphal Odes, of Pindar.   The term as applied
to English poetry is not easy to define; it carries
with it a suggestion, though sometimes only a vague
suggestion, of a public or at least a solemn occasion.
Cowper's *Boadicea*, for instance, with its prophecy
of the British Empire that is to be, is certainly an
Ode; Scott's *Rosabelle*—'O listen, listen, ladies gay'
—is as certainly not.   Generally speaking it may be
said that in the case of an Ode a performance is
conceivable; this definition is by no means adequate,
but it is sufficient for my present purpose.

The natural form of the English Ode in rhyme
has a stanza of some elaboration.   A perfect example
is the Hymn in Milton's poem, *On the Morning
of Christ's Nativity* (begun in 1629 and published

in 1645). Here performance is certainly conceivable; note the suggestion of processional movement in the pause before the final swing :—

> In consecrated earth,
>   And on the holy hearth,
> The Lars and Lemures moan with midnight plaint;
>   In urns, and altars round,
>   A drear and dying sound
> Affrights the Flamens at their service quaint;
> And the chill marble seems to sweat,
> While each peculiar power forgoes his wonted seat.
>
>   Peor and Baalim
>   Forsake their temples dim,
> With that twice-batter'd god of Palestine;
>   And mooned Ashtaroth,
>   Heaven's queen and mother both,
> Now sits not girt with tapers' holy shine;
> The Libyc Hammon shrinks his horn;
> In vain the Tyrian maids their wounded Thammuz mourn.
>
>   And sullen Moloch, fled,
>   Hath left in shadows dread
> His burning idol all of blackest hue;
>   In vain with cymbals' ring
>   They call the grisly king,
> In dismal dance about the furnace blue;
> The brutish gods of Nile as fast,
> Isis, and Orus, and the dog Anubis, haste.
>
>   Nor is Osiris seen
>   In Memphian grove or green,
> Trampling the unshower'd grass with lowings loud:
>   Nor can he be at rest
>   Within his sacred chest;
> Naught but profoundest Hell can be his shroud;
> In vain, with timbrel'd anthems dark,
> The sable-stoled sorcerers bear his worshipt ark.

V. D.   12

In such a stanza as this there is room for variation of rhythmic detail, as is seen in the case of the last line here quoted ; but the general form is most important. Observe the simplicity of structure in the stanza : the ear cannot miss the intended effect ; the rhymes satisfy expectation. Without some external assistance, such as is given by music or dancing, the comprehensive power of the ear is not very large. If the grasp is exceeded, the effect of the stanza is missed, and the composition dissolves into recitative with irregular rhymes, a form possibly legitimate, but totally different in character and capacity.

The same principle applies to variety in the length and rhythm of the verses within the stanza : the ear must be able to grasp and retain the scheme. In this respect, experiments of doubtful success have been made even by good poets. It is a question, for instance, whether the stanza of Spenser's *Epithalamion* (1595) is not too long for the ear to retain ; and if the structure is not retained, the symmetry of the repeated scheme is missed :—

> Ye learned sisters, which have oftentimes
> Beene to me ayding, others to adorne,
> Whom ye thought worthy of your gracefull rymes,
> That even the greatest did not greatly scorne
> To heare theyr names sung in your simple layes,
> But joyed in theyr praise :
> And when ye list your owne mishaps to mourne,
> Which death, or love, or fortune's wreck did rayse,
> Your string could soone to sadder tenor turne,

And teach the woods and waters to lament
Your dolefull dreriment :
Now lay those sorrowfull complaints aside ;
And having all your heads with girland crownd,
Helpe me mine owne love's prayses to resound ;
Ne let the same of any be envide :
So Orpheus did for his owne bride,
So I unto my selfe alone will sing ;
The woods shall to me answer, and my Eccho ring.

So also the irregular distribution of verses of varying length is dangerous, as being not easily followed. An illustration of this is found in Randolph's *Ode to Master Anthony Stafford* (about 1632) ; here the stanza itself is of no great length, but the irregularity in length of the verses produces a whole too complex to be easily retained by the ear :—

Ours is the sky,
Where at what fowl we please our hawk shall fly :
Nor will we spare
To hunt the crafty fox or timorous hare ;
But let our hounds run loose
In any ground they'll choose ;
The buck shall fall,
The stag and all ;
Our pleasures must from their own warrants be,
For to my Muse, if not to me,
I'm sure all game is free :
Heaven, earth, are all but parts of her great royalty.

Imitation of the ancients was the general principle of the literature of the Renaissance, and that in lyric poetry imitation should be especially of the Greek was the general assumption of English writers in the sixteenth and seventeenth centuries. But in the revival and imitation of the Greek lyric, especially of Pindar's lyric, there was a peculiar pitfall. In Greek Choric practice, music and the symmetrical movements of a company of performers are essential; the words are merely part of a larger whole. In these conditions very elaborate structures are admissible. By a strange error on the part of the scholars of the Renaissance, Pindar was supposed to be structureless, and to use an arbitrary metre which in some vague way followed the sense. Possibly this view derived encouragement from a misunderstanding of Horace's description of Pindar's dithyrambs as *numeris lege solutis* (*Carm.* IV. 2. 11) 'measures that obey no law.' But these words of Horace do not in any way imply absence of structure in Pindar's verse. Still, however we may account for the mistaken impression, there it was, and Pindar's 'sublimity' was supposed to depend on this freedom. This was a prodigious error, for Pindar's structure in respect of stanzas is peculiarly severe.

The offspring of this error is the so-called 'Pindaric' poetry of the seventeenth and eighteenth centuries, a recitative of forced irregularity both in lengths of verse and distribution of rhyme. It was thought that enough irregularity was 'sublime' *per se*, without regard to the value of single rhythms or phrases, and the result of such a theory was floods of nonsense. This subject has been amply discussed and illustrated elsewhere, and a single illustration will suffice here. Cowley is a typical, though

moderate, example of a 'Pindaric' poet. His Ode
In Praise of Pindar, written about 1645, shows
the principle, though in a comparatively moderate
form :—

I

    Pindar is imitable by none;
      The Phoenix Pindar is a vast species alone;
  Whoe'er but Daedalus with waxen wings could fly
    And neither sink too low, nor soar too high?
      What could he who follow'd claim,
    But of vain boldness the unhappy fame,
      And by his fall a sea to name?
      Pindar's unnavigable song
  Like a swoln flood from some steep mountain pours along;
    The ocean meets with such a voice
  From his enlarged mouth, as drowns the ocean's noise.

So runs the first stanza : the third I quoted in part
in my introductory lecture; the fourth begins as
follows :—

IV

    Lo, how the obsequious wind, and swelling air,
      The Theban Swan does upward bear,
    Into the walks of clouds, where he does play,
    And with extended wings opens his liquid way;...

Then with intense relief, we find Cowley leaving
the Theban Swan in the skies, and subsiding into
metre and poetry :—

    Whilst, alas, my timorous Muse
    Unambitious tracks pursues,
    Does with weak unballast wings,
    About the mossy brooks and springs,

About the trees' new-blossom'd heads,
About the garden's painted beds,
About the fields and flowery meads,
And all inferior beauteous things,
    Like the laborious bee,
For little drops of honey flee,
And there with humble sweets contents her industry.

Cowley was a very able writer, but he combined the ' Pindaric ' delusion with twists of the imagination—so-called ' conceits '—and with the unsifted vocabulary and slack composition of the pre-Dryden time. His Ode on *Christ's Passion* (printed in 1663) is nearly killed by these combined defects, but is worth study for more than one reason. The last stanza runs thus :—

Open, ah ! open wide the fountains of thine eyes,
        And let them call
    Their stock of moisture forth where'er it lies ;
        For this will ask it all ;
    'T would all, alas ! too little be
    Though thy salt tears come from a sea ;
    Canst thou deny Him this, when He
Has open'd all His vital springs for thee ?
Take heed, for by His side's mysterious flood
        May well be understood
That He will still require some waters to His blood.

All this is not to say that there may not be a legitimate use of irregular rhyme, and even of irregular rhyme combined with irregular verse, but such composition will not be an Ode, or suggest symmetrical music. It will be recitative, a perilous and difficult form, of doubtful application and very rare success, but the success when attained is

proportionately great. Of this form *Lycidas* is a
great example. In *Lycidas* the verse is almost
regular, almost uniform in its five accents. The occasional half-lines are sometimes significant, though
often arbitrary ; the rhyme, though irregular, is so
interlaced as to draw the ear on in a wandering way.
These peculiarities of form answer to the very
peculiar character of the piece ; the youthful poet
disclaims finished art, or premeditation, and must do
his best : ' bitter constraint ' compels him ; ' denial '
is ' vain '; ' thus sang the uncouth swain...with eager
thought warbling his Doric lay.' There is no
audience for the singer of Lycidas ; the work is a
meditation for a poem. Is the art conscious or
instinctive ?

As with the form, so with the subject of the
poem. There is a similar laxity of control and we
have a digression on Fame (70 ff.), and another on
the state of the Church (114 ff.). To this treatment
of the subject and to the mood of the poet the lax
form corresponds, but Milton's *Lycidas* is a thing
not to be rashly imitated.

Milton's *At a Solemn Musick* is similar in principle ; it is a silent meditation not addressed to
anyone, but exemplifying—as *Lycidas* does not—
the use of a change of rhythm to emphasise and
illustrate the thought. I quote the whole poem :—

> Blest pair of Sirens, pledges of Heaven's joy,
> Sphere-born harmonious sisters, Voice and Verse,
> Wed your divine sounds, and mixt power employ,
> Dead things with inbreath'd sense able to pierce ;

And to our high-rais'd phantasy present
That undisturbed song of pure concent,
Aye sung before the sapphire-colour'd throne
To Him that sits thereon,
With saintly shout, and solemn jubilee;
Where the bright Seraphim in burning row
Their loud up-lifted angel-trumpets blow;
And the cherubic host in thousand quires
Touch their immortal harps of golden wires,
With those just Spirits that wear victorious palms,
Hymns devout and holy psalms   15
Singing everlastingly:
That we on earth, with undiscording voice,
May rightly answer that melodious noise,
As once we did, till disproportion'd sin
Jarr'd against Nature's chime, and with harsh din
Broke the fair music that all creatures made
To their great Lord, whose love their motion sway'd
In perfect diapason, whilst they stood
In first obedience, and their state of good.
O, may we soon again renew that song,
And keep in tune with Heaven, till God ere long
To His celestial consort us unite,
To live with Him, and sing in endless morn of light!

There is only one such touch in the poem, a very
delicate one : in *vv.* 15 and 16, the rhythm of church
music is recalled by the change of accentuation :—

> Hýmns devoút and hóly psálms
> Sínging everlástingly.

The whole of this poem of Milton has been here
quoted, not only to exemplify my point of the effect
obtained by the single change of rhythm, but also
because, with that *On the Morning of Christ's*

Nativity, it gave a most important hint to Dryden for his first *Song for St Cecilia's Day*. The world, the cosmos, order, all is based on harmony, that is to say, on Music. The thought is Platonic, but its application to poetry, as well as the use of intentional variation of rhythm, was suggested to Dryden by Milton's work. Notice the coincidences of vocabulary :—

Milton.	*Dryden.*
Jarr'd against *Nature's* chime...	When *Nature* underneath a heap Of *jarring* atoms lay...
In perfect *diapason*...	The *diapason* closing full in Man.

Other interesting comparisons between the poems may be made. Milton, for instance, is much better assured than Dryden both of present touch with the Infinite and of ultimate union ; Milton dwells on the happiness of the transition, Dryden on its terror :—

> So when the last and dreadful hour
> This crumbling pageant shall devour,
> The trumpet shall be heard on high,
> The dead shall live, the living die,
> And Music shall untune the sky.

This brief sketch of Dryden's predecessors shows us what was the state of things on which he had to work. In larger lyric his course was similar to that which he took in the couplet: he instinctively avoids extravagant mistakes, works out his principles by common sense, and then suddenly—as with *Absalom and Achitophel*, so with the *Song for St Cecilia's*

Day—seizes the occasion and goes straight to the mark.

His earlier and 'Pindaric' work consists chiefly of the *Threnodia Augustalis*, written on the death of Charles II in 1685, and the *Ode to the Pious Memory of Mrs Anne Killigrew*, published in 1686. The *Threnodia* is more curious than beautiful, but contains a most interesting passage on the literary fertility and importance of the reign of Charles II, with its importation of new models, its severer standard of criticism, and its niggardly reward of poets; it is characteristic of Dryden not to omit mention of this last point in his Laureate Funeral Ode. Charles II, he says, came like spring with birds from over sea; the melodious passage (section 13) offers perhaps the only instance of thought confused to the point of unintelligibility which can be found in Dryden's works :—

> As when the new-born Phœnix takes his way
> His rich paternal regions to survey,
> Of airy choristers a numerous train
> Attends his wondrous progress o'er the plain ;
> So rising from his father's urn,
> So glorious did our Charles return ;
> The officious Muses came along,
> A gay harmonious quire, like angels ever young ;
> (The Muse that mourns him now his happy triumph sung)
> Even they could thrive in his auspicious reign ;
>   And such a plenteous crop they bore,
> Of purest and well winnow'd grain
>   As Britain never knew before ;
> Though little was their hire and light their gain,
> Yet somewhat to their share he threw ;

Fed from his hand, they sung and flew,
Like birds of Paradise that lived on morning dew.'

The confusion of metaphors for the Muses is such that the reader hesitates which of the alternative meanings should be assigned to the word 'crop'!

Dryden's *Ode to the Pious Memory of Mrs Anne Killigrew* was published in 1686 as a Preface to the poems of that lady. Anne Killigrew was an accomplished young lady who practised landscape painting as well as poetry, and was apparently very free in her imagination :—

Her pencil drew whate'er her soul design'd,
And oft the happy draught surpass'd the image in her mind.

Subsequently she produced portraits of the king and queen, James and Mary, and 'What next she had design'd, Heaven only knows.' The Ode has been praised perhaps beyond its merits from regard to the first 'stanza,' if stanza it may be called, though even this hardly deserves to be described as 'the richest complex of sounds in our language,' or in Dr Johnson's words, as 'the noblest Ode that our language ever produced' :—

Thou youngest virgin-daughter of the skies,
    Made in the last promotion of the blest ;
Whose palms, new pluck'd from Paradise,
In spreading branches more sublimely rise,
    Rich with immortal green above the rest :
Whether, adopted to some neighbouring star,
    Thou roll'st above us in thy wandering race,
    Or in procession fix'd and regular
Mov'd with the Heaven's majestic pace,

Or call'd to more superior bliss,
Thou treadst with seraphims the vast abyss :
Whatever happy region be thy place,
Cease thy celestial song a little space ;
Thou wilt have time enough for hymns divine,
Since Heaven's eternal year is thine.
Hear then a mortal Muse thy praise rehearse
    In no ignoble verse,
But such as thy own voice did practise here,
When thy first fruits of poesy were given,
To make thyself a welcome inmate there ;
   While yet a young probationer,
   And candidate of Heaven.

The effect of this section depends largely on its skilful grammatical construction ; it forms practically one unbroken sentence.   Moreover, the irregularity of rhythm is turned to purpose in the short line ' In no ignoble verse.'   On the other hand the end—the last two lines—is weak.   The general subject is not attractive ; it is clear that Dryden did not really admire the lady's art.   His rhythms, moreover, are arbitrary and confused, though not ugly.   Best in substance and form taken together is the ninth section, *pace* Scott who chooses it for special blame. The lady had a brother in the Navy who, being at sea, was for some time ignorant of her death.   The situation is a pathetic one ; the reader will remember Tennyson's description of the similar but reversed situation in *In Memoriam*, section VI :—

      ......while thy head is bow'd,
His heavy-shotted hammock-shroud
Drops in his vast and wandering grave.

Dryden writes :—

> Meantime, her warlike brother on the seas
> His waving streamers to the winds displays,
> And vows for his return with vain devotion pays.
>   Ah, generous youth! that wish forbear,
>   The winds too soon will waft thee here!
>   Slack all thy sails, and fear to come :
> Alas! thou know'st not, thou art wreck'd at home.   7
> No more shalt thou behold thy sister's face,
> Thou hast already had her last embrace.
> But look aloft, and if thou kenst from far,
> Among the Pleiads, a new-kindled star,
> If any sparkles than the rest more bright,
> 'Tis she that shines in that propitious light.

Scott objects to the introduction of the star : ' Our emotion is quelled by the nature of the consolation administered to a sea-captain, that his sister is turned into a star.' This is an objection which Dryden would have failed to understand. The association of souls with stars, illustrated in the first section of the poem—' adopted to some neighbouring star '— is a classical commonplace, but classical romance was dead to Scott. There is an instance of significant variation of the rhythm in this section, where the irregular and broken rhythm of the seventh line disappoints the expectation raised by the three smooth lines of octosyllabic verse immediately preceding.

The tenth and last section gives a version of Dryden's favourite topic, the Day of Judgement, and is interesting for the contrast which it offers to his treatment of the same subject in the close of the

Song for St Cecilia's Day.   The version in the *Ode
to the Pious Memory of Mrs Anne Killigrew* is not
free from the grotesque:—

> When in mid-air the golden trump shall sound,
>   To raise the nations under ground;
>   When in the Valley of Jehosophat
> The judging God shall close the book of Fate,
>   And there the last assizes keep
>   For those who wake and those who sleep;
>   When rattling bones together fly
>   From the four corners of the sky;
> When sinews o'er the skeletons are spread,
> Those cloth'd with flesh, and life inspires the dead;
> The sacred poets first shall hear the sound,
> And foremost from the tomb shall bound,
> For they are cover'd with the lightest ground;
> And straight, with inborn vigour, on the wing,
> Like mounting larks, to the new morning sing.
> There thou, sweet saint, before the quire shalt go,
> As harbinger of Heaven, the way to show,
> The way which thou so well hast learn'd below.

In the fourth section there is a very interesting
autobiographical parenthesis, representing Dryden's
repentance for his profligation of the Muse:—

> O gracious God! how far have we
> Profan'd thy heavenly gift of Poesy!
> Made prostitute and profligate the Muse,
> Debas'd to each obscene and impious use,
> Whose harmony was first ordain'd above,
> For tongues of angels and for hymns of love!
> O wretched we! why were we hurried down
>   This lubric and adulterate age,
> (Nay, added fat pollutions of our own,)
>   To increase the steaming ordures of the stage?

The date of these lines should be noted. The poem was published in 1686, twelve years before Jeremy Collier's attack upon Dryden and at the time of Dryden's full prosperity, when pretence of any kind was not necessary. Dryden's attitude and behaviour about this subject was never consistent, but his repentance is not a mere fiction.

If then we are to summarise the lyrical situation in 1686, we may say that it was utterly confused, and that Dryden was no better grounded than others, but was feeling his way. The way was found— found suddenly, and the arrival at the end announced the next year by the production of *A Song for St Cecilia's Day*. The occasion was the annual performance of a musical society on November 22, the festival of St Cecilia, who was the inventress of the organ and the patroness of music. The poetic products of the first years after the foundation of this society were not noticeable, but in 1687 the audience was provided with this :—

I

From harmony, from heavenly harmony
    This universal frame began ;
    When Nature underneath a heap
        Of jarring atoms lay,
        And could not heave her head,
The tuneful voice was heard from high,
        Arise, ye more than dead.
Then cold and hot and moist and dry
    In order to their stations leap,
        And Music's power obey.

From harmony, from heavenly harmony
This universal frame began :
From harmony to harmony
Through all the compass of the notes it ran,
The diapason closing full in Man.

II

What passion cannot Music raise and quell?
When Jubal struck the chorded shell
His listening brethren stood around,
And, wondering, on their faces fell
To worship that celestial sound :
Less than a god they thought there could not dwell
Within the hollow of that shell,
That spoke so sweetly, and so well.
What passion cannot Music raise and quell?

III

The trumpet's loud clangor
Excites us to arms
With shrill notes of anger
And mortal alarms.
The double double double beat
Of the thundering drum
Cries, hark ! the foes come ;
Charge, charge, 'tis too late to retreat.

IV

The soft complaining flute
In dying notes discovers
The woes of hopeless lovers,
Whose dirge is whisper'd by the warbling lute.

V

Sharp violins proclaim
Their jealous pangs and desperation,
Fury, frantic indignation,
Depth of pains and height of passion,
For the fair, disdainful dame.

VI

But oh! what art can teach,
What human voice can reach
    The sacred organ's praise?
Notes inspiring holy love,
Notes that wing their heavenly ways
    To mend the choirs above.

VII

Orpheus could lead the savage race,
And trees unrooted left their place,
    Sequacious of the lyre;
But bright Cecilia rais'd the wonder higher:
When to her organ vocal breath was given,
An angel heard, and straight appear'd
    Mistaking earth for heaven.

Grand Chorus

As from the power of sacred lays
    The spheres began to move,
And sung the great Creator's praise
    To all the blest above;
So when the last and dreadful hour
This crumbling pageant shall devour,
The trumpet shall be heard on high,
The dead shall live, the living die,
And Music shall untune the sky.

Of the connexion of the general scheme of this poem with Milton's poems *At a Solemn Musick* and *On the Morning of Christ's Nativity*, I have already spoken. The passage on the function of Music in the latter is as follows :—

    Such music (as 'tis said)
    Before was never made,

> But when of old the sons of morning sung,
>> While the Creator great
>> His constellations set,
> And the well-balanc't world on hinges hung;
> And cast the dark foundations deep,
> And bid the weltering waves their oozy channel keep.

The theory of both Milton and Dryden is that the world was created, and is held together, by harmony —that is, proportion—and that man, the microcosm, is a summary of creation, responsive to all rhythms. The world hereafter is to be resolved not into Chaos but into another and a better music. Dryden touches this subject with great awe, herein presenting a striking contrast with the attitude of Milton.

The essential merit of Dryden's poem is that he has seized the principle that variations of rhythm, if not echoed and repeated—as they are in a poem composed of stanzas—can have value only so far as they illustrate the sense; otherwise they are mere licences. This principle is not only grasped but, by the peculiar felicity of the occasion, it is perfectly realised; the theme, the power of music, allows the illustrations of sense by rhythm to be everywhere explicit.

To come to details, and consider some of the sections :—

'Pindaric' verse is not really appropriate to anything except Chaos, and the structure of the opening section is a sort of jest upon this point; for harmony —the actual word 'harmony'—brings the delayed rhyme. The first two rhymes of the section, 'harmony' and 'began,' are left suspended—for there is no true rhyme to ' harmony ' in ' high ' and ' dry '—while all the irregularly accented lines that follow one after another find their re-echoing rhymes. Only with the repetition of the two opening lines is the expectant ear fully satisfied.

In the fifth section, with his imitation of the violin, Dryden shows his supreme technical skill. The rhythmical effect is apt to be spoilt by too close an observance of the conventional division of the lines.

There is an obvious difficulty in differentiating the organ from other musical instruments, but Dryden gets a point and suggests the echo of the more remote pipes by the repetition of the word 'notes' and the recurrence of similar sounds in verses 4 and 5 :—

> Notes inspiring holy love
> Notes that wing their heavenly ways...

In the first half of the seventh section, introducing the legend of Cecilia and the angel, we have an abrupt change of language, felt in ' savage race,' —here used not of men, but in the Latin sense of ' wild beasts '[1]—and strongly emphasised in the Latinism ' sequacious of.' There is a touch of reserve, almost of humour, in Dryden's association of the two legends of Orpheus and St Cecilia.

---

[1] Cf. Lucretius v 967 'siluestria saecla ferarum,' and Virgil *Georgic* II 374 ' siluestres uri...capreaeque sequaces.'

With the Grand Chorus we return to plain language and to the solemnity of 'Common Metre,' alternate lines of eight and six syllables. The Day of Judgement, a favourite subject with Dryden, here finds its most successful treatment.

Ten years later, in 1697, on a similar occasion, Dryden applied the same principle again in *Alexander's Feast; or, The Power of Music*. A series of different musical effects as affecting and representing different passions was now by an extremely happy invention applied to a story. The story chosen rests on a slight historical foundation, the burning of the great Persian temple by Alexander and his companions under the excitement of a banquet. Dryden supposes Alexander to be led up to this action, through a chain of varied emotions, by the power of the musician Timotheus; and under the alternate stimulus and enfeeblement of wine the rapid changes required for Dryden's technical purpose are at least conceivable.

The poem is almost too familiar for comment; yet misunderstandings, or at least different understandings, of its metrical effects are certainly possible. Take for instance Young's Essay *On Lyric Poetry*, which he illustrates by two compositions of his own, *Ocean; an Ode*, and an introductory *Ode to the King*. The Essay is a feeble performance hardly deserving criticism, but a point of interest is in the following words :—

> I think Mr Dryden's Ode on St Cecilia's Day [by which he means the second ode, *Alexander's Feast*] inferior to no

composition of this kind. Its chief beauty consists in adapting the numbers [that is, the metre] most happily to the variety of the occasion. Those by which he has chosen to express majesty, (viz.)

> Assumes the god,
> Affects to nod,
> And seems to shake the spheres,

are chosen in the following ode [Young's own *Ode to Ocean*], because the subject of it is great...

and similarly in the *Ode to the King* Young chooses the same metre, presumably for the same purpose. Young then, it is clear, takes Dryden in the passage which he quotes from *Alexander's Feast* to intend and to express true sublimity ; here is the result of this assumption :—

> When rushes forth
> The frowning north
> On black'ning billows, with what dread
> My shuddering soul
> Beholds them roll,
> And hears their roarings o'er my head !
>
> With terror mark
> Yon flying bark !
> Now centre-deep descend the brave ;
> Now, toss'd on high
> It takes the sky,
> A feather on the tow'ring wave !
>
>   *   *   *   *
>
> All ether burns !
> Chaos returns !
> And blends, once more, the seas and skies :
> No space between
> Thy bosom green,
> O deep ! and the blue concave, lies.

Or again, speaking of the bottom of the sea :—

> In chambers deep,
> Where waters sleep,
> What unknown treasures pave the floor !
> The pearl, in rows,
> Pale lustre throws ;
> The wealth immense, which storms devour

These lines are of course faulty in all respects, conceptions, phrasing, grammar, but surely the metre is also absurdly inappropriate : the jigging movement is inconsistent with gravity and dignity. Young would make Dryden his authority for the choice the metre is, he says, that 'by which Dryden has chosen to express majesty.' But is this so? Let us go to Dryden's own version and see the situation. Timotheus with the help of the audience twists Alexander about, leads him a dance, not without a certain sly malice, and recounts the legend of his divine parentage. The King and the company are in the right mood for the fable :—

> The listening crowd admire the lofty sound,
> A present deity, they shout around;
> A present deity, the vaulted roofs rebound:
> With ravish'd ears
> The monarch hears,
> Assumes the god,
> Affects to nod,
> And seems to shake the spheres.

This see-saw surely does not express majesty, true dignity, but mock majesty, the self-complacency of the drop too much. To justify Young's use of Dryden's metre in his *Ode to the King*, one must suppose George II prepared for the poem as Alexander was prepared for the song of Timotheus; sober, he would hardly be uplifted by this :—

> At his proud foot
> The sea, pour'd out,
> Immortal nourishment supplies;
> Thence wealth and state,
> And power and fate,
> Which Europe reads in George's eyes.
>
> From what we view,
> We take the clue,
> Which leads from great to greater things :
> Men doubt no more,
> But gods adore,
> When such resemblance shines in kings.

Scepticism, we learn, is to be cured by observing the living reflexion of the deity in George II. This is what Young makes out of Dryden's humorous treatment of the Pagan fable, that in Alexander Jove 'stamped an image of himself'; for a Christian divine the flight is remarkable. After all, the metre is perhaps not so inappropriate, but one is disposed to pardon George for his contempt of 'bainting and boetry.'

These verses are quoted from no desire to depreciate Young, a real poet in his proper vein; but just because of his genius, his blunder proves that to acquire a true judgement of rhythm we may need some pains and possibly some mutual help. Hence the suggestions offered in the following detailed comments on a few points in *Alexander's Feast*.

I

'Twas at the royal feast for Persia won
   By Philip's warlike son:
   Aloft in awful state
   The godlike hero sate
     On his imperial throne;
His valiant peers were plac'd around;
Their brows with roses and with myrtles bound:
   (So should desert in arms be crown'd.)
The lovely Thais, by his side,
Sate like a blooming Eastern bride,
In flower of youth and beauty's pride.
   Happy, happy, happy pair,
     None but the brave,
     None but the brave,
None but the brave deserves the fair.

In the opening line 'the royal feast for Persia won' there is a dangerous Latinism, for the unobservant reader may think that it was the feast and not Persia that was won. This section illustrates the tendency to simple grouping, a tendency which becomes important in the work of Gray, but is not yet fixed in Dryden's case. Here the grouping is in triplets; there are first two sets of triple rhymes, 'around, bound, crown'd,' and 'side, bride, pride'—followed by the triple repetition of the word 'happy' and of the phrase 'none but the brave.'

The rhythm of the second section is rather confused, but the approach of Bacchus in the third is accompanied by a definite rhythmical effect produced by a series of lines of a successively diminishing number of accents (one of six, one of five, etc.), followed by a sudden expansion in the all but monosyllabic line :—

> Now give the hautboys breath, he comes, he comes.

and this is followed by diminution again.

But perhaps the cleverest touch in the whole piece is the fashion in which, in the sixth section, the rhythm dies altogether away in the description of the unburied dead :—

> Behold a ghastly band,
> Each a torch in his hand!
> Those are Grecian ghosts, that in battle were slain,
> And unburied remain
> Inglorious on the plain.

Note also the holding up of the rhythm, and the quivering beat, in the line :—

> And glittering temples of their hostile gods,

followed by the sudden return to the dactyls in :—

> The princes applaud with a furious joy.

The last four lines of the seventh section :—

> Let old Timotheus yield the prize,
> Or both divide the crown :
> He rais'd a mortal to the skies ;
> She drew an angel down.

have been criticised as making a false point in the contrast between Timotheus and St Cecilia. But the objection is of doubtful force ; the legend of St Cecilia is not treated seriously by Dryden, but lightly, as in his earlier Ode, and the 'angel' is merely the legendary visitant of the inventress of the organ.

The story that this Ode was 'finished at a sitting' rests on no good authority and I take leave to doubt its accuracy.

Probably neither Dryden's audience, nor Dryden himself, fully understood the step that had been taken; certainly Dryden himself did not maintain it. The death of Purcell, the musician, in 1695 produced two Odes: one, Mulgrave's, is a feeble and amateur performance, and the other, Dryden's own, written for a musical setting two years before the second Ode for St Cecilia's Day, presents an odd mixture of novel merits and old errors. The rhythms are confused, the changes being mostly without meaning. But there is one exquisite line in his latest style, the concluding line of the first section :—

> Mark how the lark and linnet sing:
> 　　With rival notes
> They strain their warbling throats
> 　　To welcome in the spring.
> 　　But in the close of night,
> When Philomel begins her heavenly lay,
> 　　They cease their mutual spite,
> 　　Drink in her music with delight,
> And listening and silent, silent and listening, listening and
> 　　silent, obey.

The natural history is dubious, but the picture exquisite. The rest of the Ode is rubbish: Purcell cannot be in hell, for the devils will not permit it :—

> 　　The power of harmony too well they knew;
> 　　He long ere this had tun'd their jarring sphere,
> 　　　And left no Hell below.

The third section is even worse. It begins with
a pun on the word scale, 'ladder,' as applied to
music :—

> The heavenly choir, who heard his notes from high,
> Let down the scale of music from the sky

and goes on to assure us that all other musicians are
safe from heavenly depredations, for now that the
gods have got the best they will be content. In
fact the death of Purcell is regarded as a sort of
rape of Ganymede, a conceit quite in the old style
of the days of Charles I.

In the eighteenth century elaborate lyric a-
bounded, but made little progress, so that Gray,
essaying the Pindaric Ode in 1754, can suggest that
the 'Æolian lyre' has slept since Dryden's death :—

> Behold, where Dryden's less presumptuous car
> Wide o'er the fields of glory bear
> Two coursers of ethereal race,
> With necks in thunder cloth'd, and long resounding pace.

> Hark, his hands the lyre explore !
> Bright-ey'd Fancy, hovering o'er,
> Scatters from her pictur'd urn
> Thoughts that breathe and words that burn.
> But ah 'tis heard no more—
> O lyre divine, what daring spirit
> Wakes thee now?

Akenside might very well represent the 'sleep'
of the lyre; his productions are mostly mere rhetoric.
But Akenside and Gray were considerable scholars
and they introduced into English lyric the new and

true Pindaric form of Ode, containing strophe, anti-
strophe, and epode. In this strict Pindaric form Gray
wrote the *Progress of Poesy* and *The Bard*, but the
form itself is of doubtful importance in English poetry.

Gray avowedly builds on Dryden ; he takes up
the principle, visible, as we have seen, in parts of
Alexander's Feast, of commending a long stanza to
the ear by subdividing it into sections, each section
being in itself simple and regular. This principle is
shown plainly in Gray's *Ode on the Spring*, a work
slight and of little intrinsic value. This poem, written
in 1742, is not of the Pindaric type ; it consists of six
similar stanzas of ten lines, these ten lines being
divided into groups of four and six lines respectively,
so that the rhythms and rhymes are easily followed
and remembered by the ear ; thus :—

> Lo ! where the rosy-bosom'd Hours,
>   Fair Venus' train, appear,
> Disclose the long-expecting flowers,
>   And wake the purple year !
> The Attic warbler pours her throat,
> Responsive to the cuckoo's note,
>   The untaught harmony of Spring ;
> While, whispering pleasure as they fly,
> Cool Zephyrs through the clear blue sky
>   Their gather'd fragrance fling.

The more complicated arrangement in *The Progress of Poesy* is worth analysis. The first stanza
runs as follows :—

> Awake, Æolian lyre, awake,
>   And give to rapture all thy trembling strings.
>   From Helicon's harmonious springs
> A thousand rills their mazy progress take ;

The laughing flow'rs, that round them blow,
Drink life and fragrance as they flow.
Now the rich stream of music winds along,
Deep, majestic, smooth, and strong,
Through verdant vales, and Ceres' golden reign ;
Now rolling down the steep amain,
Headlong, impetuous, see it pour :
The rocks and nodding groves rebellow to the roar.

To this 'strophe,' the second stanza, the 'anti-strophe,' corresponds. The structure is simple ; the arrangement of rhymes is easily followed, and there is little variety in the rhythms. There is more variety of rhythm in the epode (I 3) where a mass in short metre (I I lines) is followed by a mass in long metre. Note carefully that this transition is in all the three epodes (I 3, II 3, III 3) strictly adapted to an important transition in the sense, and also that in I 3 it expresses a musical change, just as the change of rhythm does in Dryden's first *Song for St Cecilia's Day*. The metre, like the music, changes when, after the Loves have been 'frisking light in frolic measures,'

Slow melting strains their Queen's approach declare.

I 3

Thee, the voice, the dance, obey,
Temper'd to thy warbled lay.
O'er Idalia's velvet green
The rosy-crowned Loves are seen
On Cytherea's day
With antic Sports and blue-eyed Pleasures,
Frisking light in frolic measures ;

> Now pursuing, now retreating,
>   Now in circling troops they meet :
> To brisk notes in cadence beating,
>   Glance their many-twinkling feet.

Then come the longer lines :—

> Slow melting strains their Queen's approach declare ;
>   Where'er she turns, the Graces homage pay.
> With arms sublime, that float upon the air,
>   In gliding state she wins her easy way :
> O'er her warm cheek, and rising bosom, move
> The bloom of young Desire and purple light of Love.

Many other similar observations on the technical merits of this poem might be made, but we must not digress far, only calling attention to the variation in Gray's treatment of the three-accented verse which makes the fifth line in each epode :—

> Ón Cytheréa's dáy—   (I 5)
>
> In língering lábyrinths créep—   (II 5)
>
> But áh ! 'tis héard no móre.   (III 5)

Gray's exquisite phrasing passes off much audacity, not to say nonsense. Thus there is a double conception of the subject : Poetry is a universal consolation—a view represented in II 1, 'Say, has he given in vain the heavenly Muse,' and Poetry is also an occasional effulgence : in II 2 we slide from one conception to the other. His 'history' again is absurd ; there are, we learn, three poetic periods, the Greek, succeeded by the Roman, which, in its turn is succeeded by the English ; and this last apparently begins with Shakespeare :—

> Till the sad Nine, in Greece's evil hour,
>   Left their Parnassus for the Latian plains.
> Alike they scorn the pomp of tyrant Power,
>   And coward Vice, that revels in her chains.
> When Latium had her lofty spirit lost,
> They sought, O Albion ! next thy sea-encircled coast.

Hence the Ode as a whole disappoints hopes raised by familiar quotations, such as the description of the mythical Shakespeare, 'Nature's Darling' (III 1), which immediately follows.

The Pindaric Ode is far better managed in *The Bard*. The problem here was to rival *Alexander's Feast* by fitting successive phases of music to the stages of a story. Gray's solution is ingenious. A Welsh bard, escaped from massacre, prophetically chants from a safe rock a series of Plantagenet disasters in defiance of Edward I, hails the Tudors as Welsh and native, and then flings himself into the river below.

The subdivision of the stanzas is more clearly defined than in *The Progress of Poesy*, and is most important. The strophe (and of course the corresponding antistrophe) has two main divisions sharply marked by metre, and each of these is further subdivided. It is the same with the epode. This system of divisions fits admirably the passage from vision to vision in prophecy ; such brevity as Gray gives us would hardly otherwise be possible. Take for instance the three first sub-stanzas in II 3, respectively consisting of six, four, and four lines, representing (*a*) the death of Richard II, (*b*) the Wars of the Roses, (*c*) Henry VI and the end of the Lancastrians.

II 3

(*a*) Fill high the sparkling bowl,
　　　The rich repast prepare,
　　　　Reft of a crown, he yet may share the feast ;
　　　Close by the regal chair
　　　Fell Thirst and Famine scowl
　　　　A baleful smile upon their baffled guest.
(*b*) Heard ye the din of battle bray,
　　　　Lance to lance, and horse to horse ?
　　　　Long years of havock urge their destin'd course,
　　　And through the kindred squadrons mow their way.
(*c*) Ye towers of Julius, London's lasting shame,
　　　With many a foul and midnight murder fed,
　　　　Revere his Consort's faith, his father's fame,
　　　And spare the meek usurper's holy head.

Or again take the subdivisions in III 1, where the third subdivision, at a point where the ear has now been led to expect change, introduces the prophecy of the coming Tudors :—

III 1

　　　Edward, lo ! to sudden fate
　　(Weave we the woof.   The thread is spun.)
　　　Half of thy heart we consecrate.
　　(The web is wove.   The work is done.)
　　Stay, oh stay ! nor thus forlorn
　　Leave me unbless'd, unpiti'd, here to mourn :
　　In yon bright track, that fires the western skies,
　　They melt, they vanish from my eyes.

Then, with the change of metre :—

> But oh! what solemn scenes on Snowdon's height
>> Descending slow their glittering skirts unroll?
> Visions of glory, spare my aching sight!
>> Ye unborn ages, crowd not on my soul!
> No more our long-lost Arthur we bewail.
> All hail, ye genuine kings, Britannia's issue, hail!

Gray's style is totally different from Dryden's; it is much more artificial, sometimes even artificial beyond the permitted limit—as, for instance, when he writes : ' Is the sable warrior fled?' But in the arrangement of sentences, the straightforward order, he is strongly influenced by Dryden, and so also in the rich use of plain words, such words as, in the last six lines quoted, *skirts, aching, crowd.*

In Collins's *Ode on the Passions* (published 1747) we have a manifest revival in a different form of the idea of Dryden's first *Song for St Cecilia's Day*; instead of the varied rhythms illustrating types of music which raise this or that passion, we have the passions themselves as persons—Despair, Hope, Fear, etc., each giving a characteristic musical performance. Hope, for instance, is interrupted by Revenge :—

> And longer had she sung;—but with a frown,
>> Revenge impatient rose:
> He threw his blood-stain'd sword in thunder down;
>> And with a withering look,
>> The war-denouncing trumpet took,
> And blew a blast so loud and dread,
> Were ne'er prophetic sounds so full of woe!
>> And ever and anon he beat
>> The doubling drum with furious heat;

And though sometimes, each dreary pause between,
　　Dejected Pity, at his side,
　　Her soul-subduing voice applied,
　Yet still he kept his wild unalter'd mien,
While each strain'd ball of sight seemed bursting from his
　　head.

Collins's variations are very good though hardly equal to Dryden's best. His poem contains an allusion to Dryden; Greek music and poetry in their varied simplicity rivalled—or rather, Collins says, surpassed—even Cecilia's Organ. Addressing Music, he asks why she has laid aside her ancient lyre :—

　　　'Tis said, and I believe the tale,
　　　Thy humblest reed could more prevail,
　　　Had more of strength, diviner rage,
　　　Than all which charms this laggard age ;
　　　E'en all at once together found,
　　　Cecilia's mingled world of sound.

Collins would revive this Greek art, but does not seem to realise the nature of the model or the difficulties of imitation. Still, when all is said, *The Passions* is a very fine poem, though not exactly an Ode—and it counts to Dryden.

All these poems, of which I have spoken, and some later poetry—for instance, much of Swinburne's—depend on adaptation of metrical variation to variations in sense. But there is a legitimate field, though the seventeenth and eighteenth centuries did not find it, for irregular and wandering metre, merely as such, and apart from the significance

of variations; such metre properly expresses
reverie, thought, not addressed to an audience but
as it were overheard. The leading example is
Wordsworth's so-called Ode, *Intimations of Immortality from Recollections of Early Childhood,*
—not an ode at all according to our definition.
Performance is inconceivable; the irregularity of
the metre, which in places is almost wild, suggests
private thought in a natural undress. It is interesting to note that Professor Jebb, whose fineness
of touch, sure dexterity, and exact comprehension
are nowhere better shown than in his rendering of
this piece, so little felt the variations in rhythm as
essential to the poem that he translated the whole
into Greek hexameters, a thing impossible in the
case of such a poem as Gray's *The Bard.* But that
metrical irregularity *on the whole* pleases cannot
always be said. In section VII, for instance, of this
poem, after describing the fondness of children for
imitating and acting, Wordsworth represents the
temporary denizen of this world as amusing himself with his part. Here the irregularity is to my
ear not pleasing :—

> See, at his feet, some little plan or chart,
> Some fragment from his dream of human life,
> Shap'd by himself with newly-learned art;
>   A wedding or a festival,
>   A mourning or a funeral;
>   And this hath now his heart,
>   And unto this he frames his song:
>   Then will he fit his tongue
> To dialogues of business, love or strife;

> But it will not be long
> Ere this be thrown aside,
> And with new joy and pride
> The little Actor cons another part;

It may be suggested that the changes of metre represent the vagrant fancy of the 'little Actor'; this idea however will not work out in detail, and to me the general effect seems of questionable success.

But on the whole the wandering measure of the poem is suitable to a reverie overheard. Wordsworth, however, seems to feel, and to feel with reason, that some definitely musical effects, some appropriate rhythms, should be sought, especially in the reverie of a poet. He has achieved this with a skill which *in this kind* he shows nowhere else. That skill he learnt from Dryden, whom he admired in spite of differences and repulsions. The following lines, from the third section, might in form be taken from Dryden :—

> And all the earth is gay;
> Land and sea
> Give themselves up to jollity,
> And with the heart of May
> Doth every Beast keep holiday!
> Thou Child of Joy,
> Shout round me, let me hear thy shouts, thou happy Shepherd-
> boy !

In section IV the rhythmical effects are not very well managed, but in section V ('Our birth is but a sleep and a forgetting'), where the note of reverie is important, there is one admirable rhythmic effect, the gay march introduced in the third and fourth lines of the following :—

> The Youth, who daily farther from the east
>   Must travel, still is Nature's Priest,
>   And by the vision splendid
>   Is on his way attended ;
>   At length the Man perceives it die away,
>   And fade into the light of common day.

3
4

But it is in the ninth section that the culminating passage is found :—

> But for those first affections,
> Those shadowy recollections,
>   Which, be they what they may,
> Are yet the fountain light of all our day,
> Are yet a master light of all our seeing ;
>   Uphold us, cherish, and have power to make
> Our noisy years seem moments in the being
> Of the eternal Silence : truths that wake,
>   To perish never ;
> Which neither listlessness, nor mad endeavour,
>   Nor Man nor Boy,
> Nor all that is at enmity with joy,
> Can utterly abolish or destroy !

Note here the debatable phrase 'nor Man nor Boy,' which is hardly sense, and note too how the passion grasps after strong language. Dryden, *given the thought*, might have written just so, and may therefore have influenced the glorious music which follows :—

> Hence in a season of calm weather,
>   Though inland far we be,
> Our Souls have sight of that immortal sea

> Which brought us hither,
> Can in a moment travel thither,
> And see the Children sport upon the shore,
> And hear the mighty waters rolling evermore.

Coleridge's elaborate lyrics have perhaps been over-praised; in his ode to France, for instance, the stanzas are complicated beyond comprehension.

In the nineteenth century, the 'Pindaric' Ode in its loose form produced little poetry of merit. Tennyson's *Ode on the Death of the Duke of Wellington* contains many fine sentences, but often falls flat. Tennyson wanted more bracing than is given by the loose form here used. A curious musical experiment is tried in section III, but it is to my ear not satisfactory :—

> Lead out the pageant: sad and slow,
> As fits an universal woe,
> Let the long long procession go,
> And let the sorrowing crowd about it grow,
> And let the mournful martial music blow;
> The last great Englishman is low.

But irregular verse as a form of meditation has had important descendants. Tennyson's *Maud*, as 'a monodrama,' is in one sense all meditation, and in the more passionate and intimate parts irregular verse with careful attention to musical effects is worked admirably. A few brief indications must here suffice. Thus, to take Part I only, in v I, 'A voice by the cedar-tree,' note how the lover falls into the rhythm of the lady's song heard in the distance :—

> Singing of men that in battle array,
> Ready in heart and ready in hand,
> March with banner and bugle and fife
> To the death, for their native land.

and the rest of this division repays careful examination of the rhythmical effects. So too does VI 3, and again note how the rhythm follows the description in IX of the glimpse and disappearance of Maud as she rides past and waves her hand :—

> Down by the hill I saw them ride,
> In a moment they were gone :
> Like a sudden spark
> Struck vainly in the night,
> Then returns the dark
> With no more hope of light.

The plain vigour combined with dignity of these last four lines would have delighted Dryden. Nor must I omit the dance music of XVII :—

> Till the red man dance
> By his red cedar-tree,
> And the red man's babe
> Leap, beyond the sea.

The exquisite dreaming of XVIII, 'I have led her home, my love, my only friend,' is more akin to Wordsworth, but the use in XXII, 'Come into the garden, Maud,' of the polka rhythm—polka, rather than valse, because of the strong beat—gradually developing till it is fully heard, is thoroughly in the spirit of Dryden's Odes for St Cecilia's Day.

Illustrations are endless, but I must not get too far away from my proper subject. I can therefore only briefly note that Swinburne, the chief elaborator of lyric in the Victorian age, takes up the formal ode, and his relations to the Drydenian succession, if any, are remote.   It was to other sources that he went for his models.   But the Drydenian line of inheritance is probably by no means finished ; some day *The Bard* may have a successor of like merit. The achievement would be enough for literary immortality.

VIII

THE STATE OF INNOCENCE; DRYDEN AND MILTON

In 1677, under the title *The State of Innocence and Fall of Man*, Dryden published a version of *Paradise Lost* as a rhymed play in five Acts, 'an Opera.' My reason for including in this course this work of Dryden's is not perhaps mainly the pleasure of reading it, though, apart from comparison with Milton, the poem is better than readable. Comparison with Milton is inevitable, and cannot even be made so as to treat Dryden fairly. The 'couplet' has been dissociated by historical development from mystery and solemnity; Milton's blank verse is established as the model and type of all such work, so that the mere imitation of Milton in couplets suggests parody. Set beside each other, for instance, the following passages in Dryden's play and in *Paradise Lost* :—

Lucifer. Is this the seat our conqueror has given,
And this the climate we must change for Heaven?
These regions and this realm my wars have got ;
This mournful empire is the loser's lot :
In liquid burnings, or on dry, to dwell,
Is all the sad variety of Hell.   (Act i, Sc. i)

This represents Milton's

> Is this the region, this the soil, the clime,...
> That we must change for Heaven? this mournful gloom
> For that celestial light? (*P. L.* 1 242)

Dryden goes on :—

> But see, the victor has recall'd, from far,
> The avenging storms, his ministers of war:
> His shafts are spent, and his tir'd thunders sleep,
> Nor longer bellow through the boundless deep.

and so recalls :—

> and ceases now
> To bellow through the vast and boundless deep.
> (*P. L.* 1 176)

Dryden again :—

> Best take the occasion, and these waves forsake,
> While time is given.—Ho, Asmoday, awake,
> If thou art he! But ah! how chang'd from him,
> Companion of my arms! how wan! how dim!

'Asmoday'!—we resent the substitution for Beelzebub, and find in it a suggestion of burlesque. Nor is the handling, in its own way, above criticism. Dryden writes, 'But *see*, the victor has recalled'; whom does Lucifer address? The parallel passage of Milton comes not before, but *after* the conversation between Satan and Beelzebub. So again Dryden's Lucifer says :—

> see on the lake
> Our troops, like scatter'd leaves in autumn, lie.

This is a reminiscence of Milton's description of the legions :—

> Thick as autumnal leaves that strow the brooks
> In Vallombrosa...... (1 302)

or like the scattered sedge of the Red Sea, 'whose waves o'erthrew Busiris and his Memphian chivalry.' We resent the impoverishment, and moreover Milton's description comes after the flight of Satan and Beelzebub to the land, where they could see the floating host. Dryden, much less appropriately, puts it before the flight.

Many such things as this may be found throughout the play, but nevertheless Dryden's piece is full of interest and worth an hour's attention, among other reasons for the following :—

(1) It makes an important part of our scanty evidence for Dryden's religious opinions in his middle life, before the theological poems, *Religio Laici* written in 1682, and *The Hind and the Panther* in 1687, and so bears upon the question of the honesty of Dryden in his conversion and in his tone towards religion after the Revolution. The position from which he came to his theological studies, if it could be discovered, is of importance. *The State of Innocence* is part of our evidence ; with the addition of *Tyrannic Love*, it is indeed the chief part. Moreover Dryden's earlier position is probably typical, and represents the position of many of his contemporaries.

(2) The circumstances of the publication of *The State of Innocence* and its dedication to the Duchess of York are illustrative of Dryden's feelings and of the literary characteristics of the age.

(3) The Preface is one of the most instructive of Dryden's Prefaces, as showing the groping and

tentative state of criticism at the time, and the Preface should not be separated from the play.

The date of the piece is between the end of 1674 and 1677. Milton's death, referred to in the Preface, was in November 1674 and the Duchess of York came to England in that year. The first known edition was in 1677[1]. The story told on the authority of Aubrey, that Milton's permission was asked by Dryden, and given in the words, 'You may tag my verses if you will,' is probably apocryphal. That the piece was written in a month, as Dryden himself says in his Preface, is not remarkable. Dryden also says that it was circulated, and largely circulated, in manuscript, 'many hundred copies.' The copies were very faulty and produced copious criticism—criticism not merely verbal—so that publication was demanded. Dryden's Preface gives an interesting glimpse of the literary clubs and society of his time.

The piece was dedicated to the Duchess of York, and this fact, which Dryden pleads as his principal motive for publication, does not preclude an early presentation in MS, and this I am inclined to presume. It is not probable that Dryden, admiring her, left her without poetic homage for three years. But publication was a more effectual compliment: 'I was desirous to lay at the feet of so beautiful and

[1] See the Introduction by Mr G. R. Noyes to his *Selected Dramas of John Dryden* (New York), p. xxxviii, footnote 5. The question of an earlier edition is not important for our purposes.

excellent a princess, a work, which, I confess, was unworthy her, but which, I hope, she will have the goodness to forgive.'   Dryden was really moved by the beauty and innocence of the Duchess; but he had nothing suitable to offer.   *The State of Innocence* suggested itself, and it is tolerable, though there may be something to 'forgive.'

The dedication however is now hardly tolerable: 'Your person is so admirable, that it can scarce receive addition, *when it shall be glorified*[1]: and your soul, which shines through it, finds it of a substance so near her own, that she will be pleased to pass an age within it, and to be confined to such a palace.' But this language, however objectionable, is not *courtly*.   Dryden speaks similarly of other virtuous ladies, such as the Countess of Abingdon in his *Eleonora*.   Familiarity with the unseen and mysterious was in his day encouraged by the religious. We feel it as profane, but it was not so meant. Dryden was moved by the spectacle of lovely virtue, and meant, as a poet, to show his feeling.

The circumstances of the publication account for the corrupt text, which thus offers some small textual problems :—

(*a*)   From the beach
  Thy well-known voice the sleeping gods will reach
  And wake the immortal sense, which thunder's noise
  Had quell'd, and lightning deep had driven within them.
                             (Act I, Sc. I)

For 'noise' and 'within them,' read *din* and *within*.

[1] The italics are the lecturer's.

(b)   Oh virgin, heaven-begot, and born of man,
       Thou fairest of thy great Creator's works!

                                        (Act ii, Sc. 2)

For 'works' read *plan*.

(c) *Luc.* Lives there, who would not seek to force his way,
       From pain to ease, from darkness to the day?
       Should I, who found the means to 'scape, not dare
       To change my sulphurous smoke for upper air?
       When I, in fight, sustain'd your Thunderer,
       And heaven on me alone spent half his war,
       Think'st thou those wounds were light? Should I not
         seek
       The clemency of some more temperate clime,
       To purge my gloom; and, by the sun refin'd,
       Bask in his beams, and bleach me in the wind.

                                        (Act iii, Sc. 1)

For 'clime' read *reek*; Lucifer contrasts the 'more temperate reek,' or vapour of earth—'Fair place, yet what is this to heaven'—with the 'sulphurous smoke' of Hell.

The metrical structure of the piece is worth some consideration; Dryden himself describes it as 'an Opera in Heroic Verse,' but, as Professor Saintsbury says in his *Life of Dryden*, it 'is not wholly in rhyme.' That statement, if taken without further explanation, would suggest more irregularity than is actually the case. The piece consists of about 1400 lines in all, of which one passage only, a consecutive series of some 60 lines, is in blank verse, concluding with a rhymed couplet (Act ii end of Scene 1, beginning with Lucifer's speech: 'Am I become so monstrous?'). The rest of the play is in rhymed couplets with the following exceptions :—

(1) 15 hemistichs or incomplete lines, of 4 or 6 syllables, instead of the usual 10, of which the following is an illustration :—

> *Asm.* Yet, not all perish'd : We defy him still,
>   And yet wage war, with our unconquer'd will.
> *Luc.* Strength may return.
> *Asm.* Already of thy virtue I partake,
>   Erected by thy voice.
> *Luc.*   See on the lake, etc.

The use of the hemistich is one of the devices commended in the *Essay of Dramatic Poesy* for relieving the monotony of rhymed verse.

(2) Three pairs of unrhymed lines, namely, those above quoted, where a correction of the final word restores the rhyme.

(3) Four single unrhymed lines. One of these (Act v Sc. 1, third speech of Eve after her second entry) rhymes with the last couplet but two; another (Act iii Sc. 1, third speech of Gabriel after his second entry) is followed by a broken line, thus :—

> *Luc.* Whoe'er expects our thanks, himself repays,
>   And seems but little, who can want our praise.
> *Gab.* What in us duty, shews not want in him ;
>   Blest in himself alone,
>   To whom no praise we, by good deeds, can add ;
>   Nor can his glory suffer from our bad.

In the two remaining cases the unrhymed lines stand between regularly rhyming couplets (Act ii Sc. 1, fifth speech of Adam, and Act iii Sc. 1, second speech of Ithuriel after his second entry).

I go on to a detailed consideration of the play. It is divided into five Acts :—

Act I. Decision of the devils to invade the new earth. The decision is taken by a cabinet council of six, not by a parliament of a thousand, as in Milton (*P. L.* 1 796).

Act II. Adam and Eve in Innocence. Lucifer on his way to the earth meets Uriel, the angel of the Sun.

Act III. Arrival of Lucifer in Paradise. Eve's dream of the Temptation. Discovery of Lucifer by the angel-guards and temporary expulsion of Lucifer.

Act IV. Raphael and Gabriel instruct Adam as to his position and powers. Temptation and sin of Eve.

Act V. Temptation and sin of Adam ; pronunciation by Raphael of the sentence of death. Vision by Adam and Eve of the future misery of the world and of the ultimate bliss of mankind in Heaven.

The stage directions for the scenery are crude. Thus Act 1 Scene 1, 'represents a Chaos or a confused Mass of Matter ; the Stage is almost wholly dark : a Symphony of warlike Music is heard for some time ; then from the Heavens (which are opened) fall the rebellious Angels, wheeling in Air, and seeming transfixed with Thunderbolts ; the bottom of the Stage being opened receives the Angels, who fall out of sight.' At a later point the Car of the Sun is introduced, and in the fourth Act a Cloud descends bearing six Angels, but the scenery

is for the most part simple.   The machinery would
not trouble the managers or the audience of the
seventeenth century.   Scott, in his Introduction, pro-
tests that the play can never have been 'intended
for representation.'   But why should there be stage-
directions if there was to be no representation?   It
does not seem clear that performance was not
contemplated.   Dryden, for instance, in his Preface
offers to explain the publication of 'an opera which
was never acted.'   There would be no point in this
remark if representation were altogether impossible,
and in any case there is no reason why Dryden
should not suppose that the piece could be produced.
Scott objects that the 'costume' of Paradise must
have excluded representation.   But we may note
that before the Fall, Dryden introduces in Eve's
dream (Act III Sc. I) 'a Woman habited like Eve';
Eve in Paradise then was 'habited' in Dryden's
view.   Nor is there any reason why he should not
so suppose; he ignores the Biblical account in many
particulars more important: there is, for instance,
no sentence of condemnation pronounced by the
Deity.

What Dryden retains is for the most part close
to Milton in form, but the substance is fundamentally
different ; thus

(*a*)   the metaphysical or philosophical assump-
tions of Milton are criticised by Dryden, and

(*b*)   the Christian solution is swept away.

This will appear from the following considerations :—

(*a*) Milton does not ignore the difficulties of supposing full responsibility in a created being, the conciliation of free-will and divine foreknowledge. The devils discuss this problem, and find 'no end, in wandering mazes lost' (*P. L.* ii 561). But Milton assumes as a matter of course that a guileless mind (a mind in a state of innocence) would be content with the position of man as stated. The brief statement in explanation made by Raphael (*P. L.* v 519 ff.), that free-will is necessary to virtue, is received by Adam with brief gratitude ; he passes on at once to request a narrative of the fall of the Angels.

Contrast the parallel scene in Dryden (Act iv Sc. 1). Gabriel and Raphael, with attendance of Angels, argue the case with Adam, who maintains a lively series of objections. Gabriel at one point loses his temper (!) and has to be reminded that Adam only wants instruction :—

Gabriel. And who but man should judge of man's free state?
Adam.   I find that I can choose to love or hate,
        Obey or disobey, do good or ill;
        Yet such a choice is but consent, not will.
        I can but choose what he at first design'd,
        For he, before that choice, my will confin'd.
Gabriel. Such impious fancies, where they entrance gain,
        Make heaven, all pure, thy crimes to pre-ordain.
Adam.   Far, far from me be banish'd such a thought,
        I argue only to be better taught.

Later on Adam makes a sharp repartee to Raphael :—

Raphael. Sufficient causes only work the effect,
        When necessary agents they respect.

> Such is not man; who, though the cause suffice,
> Yet often he his free assent denies.
> *Adam.* What causes not, is not sufficient still.

And finally Adam objects :—

> Better constrain'd to good, than free to ill.

whereupon Raphael, with brief reply closes the debate, leaving Adam utterly dissatisfied :—

> *Adam.* Hard state of life! Since heaven foreknows my will,
> Why am I not tied up from doing ill?
> Why am I trusted with myself at large,
> When he's more able to sustain the charge?
> Since angels fell, whose strength was more than mine,
> 'Twould show more grace my frailty to confine.
> Foreknowing the success, to leave me free,
> Excuses him, and yet supports not me.

If Dryden's verse and style here differ from Milton's, so does his theme. His position is that human responsibility could not be explained to a human *intelligence*, and that to suppose a state of *innocence in will* would not alter this. Acquiescence would mean not innocence, but want or inaction of reason.

(*b*) So much for Dryden's attitude towards the philosophical problem ; the Christian solution is simply omitted by him. The Miltonic expositions in Heaven (*P. L.* Books III and V) are not noticed or used. And so it is elsewhere. There is no reference whatever to the Redemption. This difference of treatment is chiefly apparent in the conclusion of the two poems. In *Paradise Lost* the future is revealed to Adam by Michael in a series

15—2

of visions and prophecies; Dryden follows upon
Milton's lines, only adding the presence of Eve—
who is decidedly less suppressed in Dryden's play
than in Milton's poem—and replacing Michael by
Raphael.   But the parallel form only exhibits the
discrepancy of substance.   By Milton the whole
Biblical history is shown in summary, both the Old
and the New Testament, down to the persecution
of the nascent Church, and including therefore the
story of Christ and the plan of Redemption.

Now see Dryden's conclusion.   After visions of
Death—compared below with Milton's—Raphael
speaks :—

> Death you have seen: now see your race revive,
> How happy they in deathless pleasure live ;
> Far more than I can show, or you can see,
> Shall crown the blest with immortality.

*Here a Heaven descends full of Angels and Blessed Spirits
with soft Music, a Song and Chorus.*

Adam.   Oh, goodness infinite ! whose heavenly will
> Can so much good produce from so much ill !
> Happy their state !
> Pure, and unchang'd, and needing no defence
> From sins, as did my frailer innocence.
> Their joy sincere, and with no sorrow mixt :
> Eternity stands permanent and fixt,
> And wheels no longer on the poles of Time ;
> Secure from fate, and more secure from crime.

There is no suggestion of means or conditions
by which Heaven can be attained.   It is a consoling
and reassuring imagination, bringing Creation to
the point desired and presumably intended in the

scheme. The course pursued, of which we see a stage, must be accepted by human intelligence as inexplicable.

To what Adam has said, Eve adds the following words :—

> Ravish'd with joy, I can but half repent
> The sin, which heaven makes happy in the event.

The remark is perhaps not felicitous, though natural. It is needless to suppose that Dryden did not perceive this. Discretion is not woman's strong point. In insisting on separation from Adam, Milton's Eve is not discreet, though innocent (*P. L.* IX 270 ff.). Dryden makes the scene more natural than Milton dares do. In Milton's version one does not see why Adam gives way, so careful is Milton to save the sweetness of Eve. Dryden's conception of innocence is less artificial.

But perhaps the most striking contrast with Milton's attitude is found in Dryden's final words. After encouragement from Raphael and farewells to Paradise from Adam and Eve, the piece concludes with the following fine passage :—

> *Raphael.* The rising winds urge the tempestuous air :
> And on their wings deformed winter bear ;
> The beasts already feel the change ; and hence
> They fly to deeper coverts, for defence :
> The feebler herd before the stronger run ;
> For now the war of nature is begun :
> But, part you hence in peace, and, having mourn'd your sin
> For outward Eden lost, find Paradise within.

Dryden's play is not addressed to real Christians. Theologically Milton's spirit is not altogether Christian ; it is not humble enough.   But his creed is Christian.   Dryden, on the other hand, accepts from Christianity the Resurrection and Paradise as necessary, but conceives all explanation and account of the scheme as a gratuitous embarrassment.

The State of Innocence is a translation of *Paradise Lost*, revised and adapted to a large part of society. The Duchess of York, to whom it was dedicated, was herself a Roman Catholic, and Dryden probably assumed that she would not follow very precisely and would fill up his gaps with her own comment. Dryden intends no disrespect to *Paradise Lost* ; there are very strong expressions of admiration for Milton and of deference to him in the Preface.   The Preface is better evidence for his admiration of Milton than is the nonsensical epigram which appeared under the engraving of Milton's picture, published in 1688 :—

> Three poets, in three distant ages born,
> Greece, Italy, and England did adorn.
> The first, in loftiness of thought surpass'd ;
> The next in majesty ; in both, the last.
> The force of Nature could no further go ;
> To make a third, she join'd the former two.

But Dryden did not, even in his latest years, think Milton above criticism.   In his Essay on Satire, for instance, published in 1693, he expresses the view that Milton had followed Scripture too far for

advantage of style ; *The State of Innocence* implies
the same view as regards subject-matter.

As to the style, Dryden defends heroic poetry—
under which he would class both Milton's work and
his own—in dealing with gigantic character, against
those who plead for 'imitation of Nature' as a reason
for refusing heights of imagination.   Here we come
against the old fallacy of Renaissance criticism, that
imitation is exact copying.   Dryden, however, does
not here strike the fallacy, nor indeed generally
anywhere else in his critical writings.   As to the
' machinery' of both pieces, the supernatural agents
and immaterial beings, Dryden prudently avoids
saying that his immaterial beings are real.   Milton
partly evades difficulties by dexterously avoiding
awkward juxtapositions : his 'seraph wing'd' Angel,
for instance, is material enough to *eat* when with
man 'with keen despatch of real hunger.'   Further
questions are indicated but not solved, and in
general, Milton's Heaven and cosmic setting are at
bottom confused.   We feel this, and so long as we
are not affronted by discrepancies, we accept it as a
symbol of mystery.

Dryden's tone, his determination to keep his
feet on the ground, will not allow this sort of defence.
His Uriel and other figures are only gigantic, not
mysterious.   In the Preface he avoids direct discussion of the point, falls back on Shakespeare's
Tempest and other plays, and meets the difficulty
about imitation by a strange quibble :—Fairies,
though they do not exist, are believed in ; thus

Shakespeare *imitates*, not indeed actual reality, but the real fairies of rustics. We have here an interesting proof of the difficulty there is in clearing thought. The merits of Ariel are not dependent on the fact that *someone* had or might have believed him, as described by Shakespeare, to have really existed. And Dryden himself adds, citing the Angels of Scripture and the gods of Homer, that 'thus we have notions of things above us, by describing them like other beings more within our knowledge,' and does not see that this covers the case of Ariel.

Incidentally, while on this subject, we may note that Dryden's reference, in the Preface, to Lucretius' use of the word 'image' shows that he does not understand the theory of the Epicurean *imago*.

Elevation of language, figures of style, are also defended in the Preface. On this subject Dryden is lively and amusing; he wishes that his 'imaging' were bolder, more Miltonic, and defends the four lines attacked by his critics :—

> Seraph and Cherub, careless of their charge,
> And wanton, in full ease now live at large:
> Unguarded leave the passes of the sky,
> And all dissolv'd in hallelujahs lie.

The objector, he tells us, compares with the last line anchovies dissolved in sauce. In answer he cites Virgil (*Aen.* II 265) *invadunt urbem, somno vinoque sepultam*, 'they break into the city buried in sleep and wine'; but is the case parallel ? He also cites Cowley's line, 'Where their vast courts the mother waters keep,' asking whether the metaphor must be pressed and whether 'the little waters, their daughters, make courtesy to them.' He takes his own expression, 'dissolv'd in hallelujahs,' as exactly similar to the phrase 'dissolv'd in songs of triumph.' But is this so? Legates and Tribunes might be dissolved in songs of triumph, but we cannot disregard the associations of the Hebrew words, nor the meaning of Hallelujah, a song, not of triumph, but of praise to God :—

> 'Great are thy works, Jehovah!'...
> So sung they, and the empyrean rung
> With hallelujahs : thus was sabbath kept.
>> (*P. L.* v 602, 634 f.)

He also discusses the treatment of the gigantic, citing Virgil's Polyphemus (*Aen.* III 664) :—

> Graditurque per aequor
> Iam medium ; necdum fluctus latera ardua tinxit.

'He walks through the sea up to his middle ; yet the waves wash not his high flanks' : and Cowley's Goliath, of whom Cowley writes :—

> The valley, now, this monster seemed to fill ;
> And we, methought, look'd up to him from our hill.

Dryden's apology for Cowley is ineffective and we sympathise with Scott's mutter in his note : ' With all this mitigation, the passage seems horrible bombast.' Now we touch the point. Polyphemus is much bigger than Goliath. Consider their respective stories. Ulysses did not fight Polyphemus man to man, in single combat, as David fought Goliath. Polyphemus is a monster, Goliath only a huge man ;

language poetically appropriate to a monster is bombastic if applied to a large man.

Dryden, as he is well aware, is not as bold in language as Milton, but claims a nobility of his own kind and suited to his purpose.   He disclaims the raptures of Lee's *Commendatory Verses*.   Lee wrote that Milton had given 'ore' which Dryden had 'refined'; that Milton had captured the 'rustic maid' and that Dryden had 'dressed her' and brought her 'to court'!   But Dryden doubtless saw nothing absurd in Lee's addressing him as 'awful poet.'   He would not have admitted a universal inferiority to Milton.   Nor indeed need he.   Let us compare the two poets in their treatment of the vision of Death :—

Paradise Lost XI 477 ff., the Lazar-house :—

> Immediately a place
> Before his eyes appear'd, sad, noisome, dark,
> A Lazar-house it seem'd, wherein were laid
> Numbers of all diseas'd; all maladies
> Of ghastly spasm, or racking torture, qualms
> Of heart-sick agony, all feverous kinds,
> Convulsions, epilepsies, fierce catarrhs,
> Intestine stone and ulcer, cholic pangs,
> Demoniac frenzy, moping melancholy
> And moon-struck madness, pining atrophy,
> Marasmus, and wide-wasting pestilence,
> Dropsies, and asthmas, and joint-racking rheums.
> Dire was the tossing, deep the groans; Despair
> Tended the sick busiest from couch to couch;
> And over them triumphant Death his dart
> Shook, but delay'd to strike though oft invok't
> With vows, as their chief good, and final hope.

Battles and other forms of Death are shown in later visions, but this first vision gives the typical style.

The State of Innocence, Act v Sc. 1.

The Scene shifts, and discovers deaths of several sorts. A Battle at Land and a Naval Fight.

Adam.   O wretched offspring! O unhappy state
      Of all mankind, by me betray'd to fate!
      Born, through my crime to be offenders first;
      And, for those sins they could not shun, accurst.
Eve.   Why is life forc'd on man, who, might he choose,
      Would not accept what he with pain must lose?
      Unknowing, he receives it; and when, known,
      He thinks it his, and values it, 'tis gone.
Raphael. Behold of every age; ripe manhood see,
      Decrepit years, and helpless infancy:
      Those who, by lingering sickness, lose their breath;
      And those who, by despair, suborn their death.
      See yon mad fools, who for some trivial right,
      For love, or for mistaken honour, fight:
      See those, more mad, who throw their lives away
      In needless wars; the stakes which monarchs lay,
      When for each other's provinces they play.
      Then, as if earth too narrow were for fate,
      On open seas their quarrels they debate:
      In hollow wood they floating armies bear;
      And force imprison'd winds to bring them near.

In Milton's description there is too much art, he overlays the horror. If we ask which picture is the sadder, we must answer, that it is surely Dryden's.

An interesting comparison may be made between Milton's Satan and Dryden's Lucifer. Satan has

been called the 'hero of *Paradise Lost.*' Dryden
feels this and wishes to lower him. The Devil
should, in his view, be in some sort contemptible.
It is consistent with this feeling that he suggests a
comparison between the Council in Hell and the
Dutch Republic!

> Most high and mighty lords, who better fell
> From heaven, to rise *states-general* of hell.

Milton's Satan takes the lead, both in the suggestion to assail man (*P. L.* I 655 ff.), in which he
is followed by Beelzebub at the Council (*P. L.* II
345 ff.), and in the enterprise itself (*P. L.* II 430).
In Dryden's play the counsel comes from Asmoday,
and the first offer from the 'rash Moloch,' whom
Lucifer has to check (Act I Sc. I). This difference
of attitude towards the Devil is to be remembered
in comparing the treatment of the 'dream of Eve'
by Milton and by Dryden, a passage where Dryden
most offends modern taste. The stately story is
told by Milton in the Fifth Book of *Paradise Lost*,
beginning, 'Now Morn her rosy steps in the eastern
clime Advancing sow'd the earth with orient pearl,'
and ending with 'the gracious signs of sweet remorse
And pious awe, that fear'd to have offended' (*P. L.* v
1–135). Dryden's version, given about the middle
of the Third Act, begins with Lucifer's remark,
'So, now they lie secure in love,' and ends with the
chorus of Dream-Angels singing :—

> To the joy that's forbidden we eagerly move;
> It enhances the price, and increases the love.

In this scene, Dryden has deliberately vulgarised everything, holding that the art of the Devil *is* vulgar. To Dante, to name a writer of widely differing temper and outlook, such a treatment of the Devil would have been quite intelligible.

IX

ALL FOR LOVE; OR THE WORLD WELL LOST

THE play of *All for Love; or the World Well Lost* was produced in 1677 and published the next year. It is a combination of English tradition and 'classic' rules, written in blank verse, unlike the heroic plays, and with characters forcible rather than stately: it is indeed a direct imitation of Shakespeare's *Antony and Cleopatra*. It specially deserves the attention of students of Dryden, as being the only play—so he tells us nearly twenty years later—which he 'writ for' himself.

The 'classic' rules were observed with strictness. Dryden writes in the Preface :—

> The fabric of the play is regular enough, as to the inferior parts of it; and the unities of time place and action more exactly observed than perhaps the English theatre requires. Particularly, the action is so much one that it is the only of the kind without episode, or underplot; every scene in the tragedy conducing to the main design, and every act concluding with a turn of it.

In this quotation I have followed the punctuation, Dryden's own, which is given in the recent edition of *Selected Dramas of John Dryden* by Mr G. R. Noyes[1]. But I note a mispunctuation in one sentence, which, with the ordinary punctuation, is not intelligible; for clearness, a pause should be marked after the word 'only,' and the sentence should read :—

> Particularly, the action is so much one that it is the only, of the kind without episode or underplot.

What Dryden means is that all the scenes are *parts* of one story, not (as in underplots) merely united with the main story by some connexion : such might be 'one action' in a sense, but not 'the only.' He is not claiming that no other play without episode or underplot has ever been written, but that this play is of that kind.

In *All for Love* Dryden follows in the main the traditions of the Greek and of the French stage. Each act is a single continuous scene ; the time of the action is within the limit of 'a day ;' but the place changes at least once, from the Temple of Isis in Act 1 to the Palace of Cleopatra in the remaining Acts. The play, it may be said, makes no very severe impression of the brevity of the time in which the events described occur. But clearly it shows only the last stages of a story, and fulfils the condition in which such an arrangement is easiest, by presenting us with a story that is notorious. Such was the regular practice in the Greek theatre.

Mr Noyes' Introduction on 'Dryden as a Dramatist' should be read by students of Dryden's work.

[1] See above, p. 220, note.

Writing of *All for Love* he says that 'in it many traits of the heroic plays still survive' and he thinks, though here I hardly agree with him, that in Antony there is something of Almanzor (in *The Conquest of Granada*). Dryden's Cleopatra as compared with Shakespeare's 'loses her intellectual brilliancy and her "infinite variety" and becomes a fond and faithful mistress,' for without constancy she would not be heroic or fit for tragedy: 'according to the conventions of the time, no tragic heroine must be guilty of inconstancy.' In that case we must not count as a tragic heroine the fickle Lyndaraxa of *The Conquest of Granada*. Mr Noyes quotes, with agreement, Dryden's own admission that the introduction of Octavia is a mistake, as dividing the interest of the play and diverting compassion from Antony and Cleopatra. Whether this criticism is just we will consider later, only here noting that the contemporary critics had not apparently taken the objection and that therefore Dryden had a happy opportunity to be modest without making any concession to their views.

In the Antony of Dryden, as contrasted with Shakespeare's Antony, says Mr Noyes, there is no real struggle between his infatuation for Cleopatra and his 'Roman thoughts.' This is in the main true, but does not make the action, 'as Aristotle would call it, "episodic."' Discussion of the point is better deferred till after analysis of the play.

Act I

The first Act opens in the Temple of Isis, where the prodigies that foretell the impending fall of Egypt are described by the Egyptian priests to the eunuch Alexas in a hyperbolical passage. Alexas would discard Antony and so save Egypt, but Cleopatra's love makes this impossible. Egypt's security therefore depends on a last effort of Antony. Will he make this effort? He has retired from Cleopatra for some days and the Egyptians fear that he is either hopeless or treacherous.

Ventidius then enters, Antony's 'great lieutenant in the East,' himself a Roman. His arrival 'bodes ...ill to' Egyptian affairs. He insists on seeing Antony. It is Antony's birthday and the Egyptians have proclaimed a public holiday in his honour, but Ventidius disdainfully dissociates himself from 'this general joy.' The Egyptians retire as Antony, wishing to be alone, approaches. Ventidius refuses to keep away but 'withdraws' to observe him.

Antony's first words show his melancholy; Ventidius thereupon declares himself, and both friends are moved to tears at the meeting. Ventidius encourages Antony to self-reproach, and then discloses a new hope: twelve legions are ready for Antony in a place described, with geographical vagueness, as 'Lower Syria' (345), though apparently they have been led 'down from the Parthian marches to the Nile' (340). But these legions will not fight for Cleopatra, so that Antony must first break with her. At this Antony is angry, inveighs furiously against the 'plain insolence' of Ventidius and calls him a traitor. This accusation Ventidius indignantly disproves and Antony retracts it.

The scene is good and finely written; it should be read as a whole, and is too long to quote. But I would draw special attention to the 60 lines from *v.* 359, where Ventidius begins his attack upon Cleopatra, to the complete conversion of Antony, concluding thus[1]:—

Ant. Thou only lov'st, the rest have flatter'd me.
Vent. Heav'n's blessing on your heart for that kind word!
      May I believe you love me? Speak again.
Ant. Indeed I do. Speak this, and this, and this.   417
                                 [*Hugging him.*]
      Thy praises were unjust; but I'll deserve 'em,
      And yet mend all. Do with me what thou wilt;
      Lead me to victory! thou know'st the way.

I have reproduced in *v.* 417 the ordinary punctuation of all the editions. But the sense as well as the grammar would be improved by a small change avoiding the suggestion that 'Speak' is addressed to Ventidius, thus: 'Indeed I do,—speak this, and this, and this (*hugging him*).'

Act II

The action here apparently takes place in front of Cleopatra's palace where Antony and the soldiers might naturally pass. The front of the palace is

---

[1] The quotations follow the text and punctuation of Mr Noyes' Edition.

not however suitable to all the succeeding scenes and, as usual, the observance of the 'unity of place' is rather superficial.

Cleopatra, desperate but still devoted to Antony, has asked for an interview; her woman Charmion returns and reports his doubtful behaviour :—

> I told my message,
> Just as you gave it, broken and disorder'd;
> I number'd in it all your sighs and tears;
> And while I mov'd your pitiful request,
> That you but only begg'd a last farewell,
> He fetch'd an inward groan; and ev'ry time
> I nam'd you, sigh'd, as if his heart were breaking,
> But shunn'd my eyes, and guiltily look'd down:
> He seem'd not now that awful Antony,
> Who shook an arm'd assembly with his nod;
> But, making show as he would rub his eyes,
> Disguis'd and blotted out a falling tear.
>
> *Cleo.* Did he then weep? And was I worth a tear? (57 ff.)

Alexas takes encouragement from this, or rather pretends to do so, and obtains Cleopatra's leave to stop Antony on his passage, if possible. Antony, Ventidius, and 'other Commanders' then enter. In certain parts of the conversation between Antony and Ventidius, who discuss the character of Octavius (Caesar Augustus), it is impossible not to see allusions to Louis XIV; thus, Antony says :—

> If he ventures
> (As in Illyria once they say he did,
> To storm a town), 'tis when he cannot choose;
> When all the world have fix'd their eyes upon him;
> And then he lives on that for seven years after;
>
> (114 ff.)

16—2

and again :—

> He would live, like a lamp, to the last wink,
> And crawl upon the utmost verge of life.
> O Hercules ! why should a man like this,
> Who dares not trust his fate for one great action,
> Be all the care of heav'n?   (129 ff.)

Louis XIV, as Macaulay writes in the *Essay on Sir William Temple*, 'never repaired to a siege till it had been reported to him by the most skilful officers in his service that nothing could prevent the fall of the place. When this was ascertained, the monarch...declared the capitulation...and then returned to Versailles to hear his flatterers repeat that Turenne had been beaten at Mariendal, that Condé had been forced to raise the siege of Arras, and that the only warrior whose glory had never been obscured by a single check was Louis the Great[1].'

Alexas brings jewels for the departing Romans and the gift for Antony is a bracelet which neither he nor Alexas can fasten, so that Cleopatra is sent for to tie it on. At her entry Antony tells his whole

---

[1] See Saint-Simon's *Memoirs* I 10 for Louis' 'goût des sièges, pour y montrer sa bravoure à bon marché.' In I 3 Saint-Simon describes how in the spring of 1676—a year before the performance and two years before the publication of *All for Love*— the French army, commanded by Louis, was in close touch with the Dutch enemy under the Prince of Orange, but in spite of superiority of numbers and the advice of his generals, Louis XIV personally decided against any engagement; at the Council of war the King 'tourna bride, et il ne fut plus question de bataille,' to the great surprise of the Prince of Orange, as Saint-Simon relates at some length.

story, as a justification for his present intention, commanding her to be silent till he has finished. But his memories weaken him, and after Cleopatra has justified herself by pleading her love, the crisis comes when Antony laments for both :—

Ant.   We're both unhappy ;
          If nothing else, yet our ill fortune parts us.
          Speak ; would you have me perish by my stay?
Cleo.   If, as a friend, you ask my judgement, go ;
          If, as a lover, stay. If you must perish—
          'Tis a hard word—but stay.   (378 ff.)

Ventidius, misunderstanding, declares that Cleopatra would make a separate peace if she could. Then Cleopatra plays her trump card : she has had from Octavius an offer of a separate peace, and has refused it. Antony, blinded and overcome, retorts upon Ventidius in his own phrases :—

Ant.   My queen's not only innocent, but loves me.
          This, this is she, who drags me down to ruin !
          But, could she scape without me, with what haste
          Would she let slip her hold, and make to shore,
          And never look behind !
          Down on thy knees, blasphemer as thou art,
          And ask forgiveness of wrong'd innocence.
Vent. I'll rather die, than take it.   Will you go?
Ant.   Go ! whither? Go from all that's excellent !
          Faith, honour, virtue, all good things forbid
          That I should go from her, who sets my love
          Above the price of kingdoms.   Give, you gods,
          Give to your boy, your Cæsar,
          This rattle of a globe to play withal,
          This gewgaw world, and put him cheaply off :
          I'll not be pleas'd with less than Cleopatra. (430 ff.)

Hereupon the plan is changed, and Antony will surprise Caesar by a sortie. This sortie takes place between Act ii and Act iii, and in it five thousand Romans are killed. The proceeding is rather abrupt, but the 'unity of time' must be preserved.

Act III

The third Act opens with the return of the victorious Antony, who is met by Cleopatra. The rhodomontade which follows recalls the style of the heroic plays, but such traces are rare—and here perhaps not out of place :—

Ant.　My brighter Venus !
Cleo.　　　　　　　　O, my greater Mars !
Ant.　Thou join'st us well, my love !
　　　Suppose me come from the Phlegræan plains,
　　　Where gasping giants lay, cleft by my sword,
　　　And mountain-tops par'd off each other blow,　　15
　　　To bury those I slew.

In *v.* 15 I follow Mr Noyes, Scott, and the Quartos in reading 'par'd' (sliced off), and not 'pair'd' (coupled), which is the reading of Mr Saintsbury both in the Mermaid Edition and also in his revision of Scott's Edition.

Ventidius enters and is sneered at by Alexas, but defended good-humouredly by Antony. The procession departs, but Ventidius persuades Antony to give him an interview, and then suggests negotiation with Caesar. Antony says that for this there is no chance, as he has no instrument. He once had such an instrument in Dolabella, a devoted

friend, but they had parted on the conviction of
Antony—a just suspicion—that Dolabella loved
Cleopatra.   Dolabella is now in Caesar's camp and,
so Antony supposes, utterly estranged from him.
In the conversation Antony is the first to name
Dolabella but it was Ventidius who led him to the
recollection.   Antony's description of the friendship
is worth quoting :—

Ant.   The wretched have no friends.—
       Yet I had one, the bravest youth of Rome,
       Whom Cæsar loves beyond the love of women :
       He could resolve his mind, as fire does wax ;
       From that hard rugged image melt him down,
       And mould him in what softer form he pleas'd.
Vent. Him would I see ; that man of all the world ;
       Just such a one we want.
Ant.   He lov'd me too ;
       I was his soul ; he liv'd not but in me :
       We were so clos'd within each other's breasts,
       The rivets were not found that join'd us first.
       That does not reach us yet : we were so mix'd,
       As meeting streams,—both to ourselves were lost ;
       We were one mass ; we could not give or take,
       But from the same ; for he was I, I he.   (83 ff.)

Ventidius assures Antony of Dolabella's fidelity ;
he has in fact 'sent a messenger' with honourable
offers from Caesar.   Antony consents to receive the
messenger and Dolabella himself appears, to his
uncontrollable pleasure.   Antony is ashamed of his
reduced condition ; Dolabella and Ventidius both
confirm his self-reproach, but when Dolabella glances,
very distantly, at Cleopatra, Antony is instantly sus-
picious though he keeps a rallying tone :—Dolabella

knows that he himself was no more proof against
Cleopatra than Antony had been ; why, he gave up
his vengeance for his brother at sight of her.   This
introduces the description of Cleopatra's barge, a
direct imitation from Shakespeare.   A comparison
of the two passages I defer for the present.

Dolabella leads round the conversation to his
purpose; he has done his best for Antony with
Caesar and now brings honourable offers, procured
by a friend not named.   Antony, much moved, asks
to see the 'man,' and Ventidius produces—Octavia
and her children!   The movement of this scene is
very ingenious :—

Ant.   Show me that man,
Who has preserv'd my life, my love, my honour;
Let me but see his face.
Vent.   That task is mine,
And, Heav'n, thou know'st how pleasing.
Dol.   You'll remember
To whom you stand oblig'd?
Ant.   When I forget it,
Be thou unkind, and that's my greatest curse.
My queen shall thank him too.
Dol.   I fear she will not.
Ant. But she shall do't. The queen, my Dolabella!
Hast thou not still some grudgings of thy fever?
Dol. I would not see her lost.
Ant.   When I forsake her,
Leave me my better stars! for she has truth
Beyond her beauty. Cæsar tempted her,
At no less price than kingdoms, to betray me ;
But she resisted all: and yet thou chid'st me
For loving her too well. Could I do so?
Dol. Yes; there's my reason,...   (223 ff.)

and Ventidius brings in Octavia. Octavia offers
her 'duty' and asks nothing :—

> I'll tell my brother we are reconcil'd ;
> He shall draw back his troops, and you shall march
> To rule the East : I may be dropp'd at Athens ;
> No matter where. I never will complain,
> But only keep the barren name of wife,
> And rid you of the trouble. (300 ff.)

Antony refuses this cold bounty, being determined to force Octavia to say that she loves him ;
and this Octavia in effect confesses :—

Ant.   Then I must be oblig'd
> To one who loves me not : who, to herself,
> May call me thankless and ungrateful man :—
> I'll not endure it ; no.

Vent. (aside)   I'm glad it pinches there.

Oct.   Would you triumph o'er poor Octavia's virtue?
> That pride was all I had to bear me up ;
> That you might think you ow'd me for your life,
> And ow'd it to my duty, not my love.
> I have been injur'd, and my haughty soul
> Could brook but ill the man who slights my bed.

Ant.   Therefore you love me not.

Oct.   Therefore, my lord,
> I should not love you.

Ant.   Therefore you would leave me?

Oct.   And therefore I should leave you—if I could. (319 ff.)

The reconciliation is complete ; Octavia and the
children carry off Antony just in time for Alexas
to witness their departure. Ventidius mocks him,
and in despair and disgust Alexas admits defeat :—

> This downright fighting fool, this thick-skull'd hero,
> This blunt unthinking instrument of death,
> With plain dull virtue has outgone my wit. (379 ff.)

Cleopatra, already informed of Antony's decision and abandoning all hope, then enters, and is followed by Octavia, apparently brought by curiosity; her movements are not very clearly explained, but the stage-excitement would carry this off. There is a defiant meeting between the two; mere bitterness and fury are shown on both sides, but the scene is not undignified. Cleopatra has the best of the interview, being ashamed of nothing and shunning no exposure. Octavia leaves abruptly with a threat, and then Cleopatra breaks down. Alexas spies a hope, but Cleopatra is beyond consolation and the Act closes, as usual upon a couplet :—

> There I till death will his unkindness weep;
> As harmless infants moan themselves asleep.

Act IV

Antony sends Dolabella to carry his farewell to Cleopatra, insisting that only Dolabella can be trusted to do this gently, but Dolabella is unwilling, for he knows his own secret wishes, and desires to be loyal :—

Dol.   I should speak
So faintly, with such fear to grieve her heart,
She'd not believe it earnest.
Ant.   Therefore,—therefore
Thou only, thou art fit. Think thyself me;
And when thou speak'st, (but let it first be long),
Take off the edge from every sharper sound,
And let our parting be as gently made,
As other loves begin: wilt thou do this?   (15 ff.)

Dolabella accepts, and in a soliloquy—one of the better known passages of the play—determines to speak for himself :—

> Men are but children of a larger growth;
> Our appetites as apt to change as theirs,
> And full as craving too, and full as vain;
> And yet the soul, shut up in her dark room,
> Viewing so clear abroad, at home sees nothing;
> But, like a mole in earth, busy and blind,
> Works all her folly up, and casts it outward
> To the world's open view: thus I discover'd,
> And blam'd the love of ruin'd Antony;
> Yet wish that I were he, to be so ruin'd.   (43 ff.)

Ventidius enters and overhears Dolabella's misgivings, and being still doubtful of Antony's resolution, decides to expose Cleopatra's anticipated faithlessness.

Meanwhile Alexas, whose hope is still to save Egypt by means of Antony, prompts Cleopatra to *pretend* an intrigue with Dolabella as a means of recovering Antony by jealousy. Cleopatra very unwillingly consents to the deceit, after a characteristic taunt :—

> Can I do this? Ah, no; my love's so true,
> That I can neither hide it where it is,
> Nor show it where it is not. Nature meant me
> A wife; a silly, harmless, household dove,
> Fond without art, and kind without deceit;
> But fortune, that has made a mistress of me,
> Has thrust me out to the wide world, unfurnish'd
> Of falsehood to be happy.   (89 ff.)

Thus all converges to a love-scene between

Dolabella and Cleopatra. At their meeting Dolabella overdoes his part and represents Antony as
furious against Cleopatra; thereupon she can act
no more, faints, and when Dolabella tells her the
truth, begs him to procure her a meeting with
Antony.

Ventidius brings Octavia, who sees just enough
to make her think that Cleopatra is really false to
Antony, and Octavia and Ventidius, when left alone,
agree to reveal this to Antony, as a ground for
crushing Cleopatra and not including her in the
general peace. They think that if Antony believes
Cleopatra inclined to Dolabella, he will abandon her
finally; while Alexas thinks that jealousy will revive
Antony's love. Ventidius and Octavia tell their
story to Antony, who is furious and incredulous, to
the disgust of Octavia. Alexas, putting himself in
the way, is seized by Ventidius and 'compelled' to
confirm the truth of Ventidius' account. Alexas,
having his own theory as to the probable effect on
Antony—a return to Cleopatra, produced by jealousy,
—gives his testimony with pretended unwillingness.
The situation is good and well carried through. It
ends in the violent dismissal of Alexas, for Antony
'can bear no more.' Ventidius is much delighted,
but instantly overthrown by an explosion between
Antony and Octavia, followed by the departure of
Octavia, to the despair of Ventidius :—

Oct.   So, take my last farewell; for I despair
To have you whole, and scorn to take you half.

[*Exit*]

Vent. I combat heav'n, which blasts my best designs :
    My last attempt must be to win her back ;
    But O ! I fear, in vain.   *[Exit]*

Antony really means to break with Cleopatra, but, as he says, cannot disguise from Octavia what it costs him :—

    Why was I fram'd with this plain, honest heart,
    Which knows not to disguise its griefs and weakness,
    But bears its workings outward to the world?
    I should have kept the mighty anguish in,
    And forc'd a smile at Cleopatra's falsehood:
    Octavia had believ'd it, and had stay'd.
    But I am made a shallow-forded stream,
    Seen to the bottom: all my clearness scorn'd,
    And all my faults expos'd !   (427 ff.)

Dolabella and then Cleopatra now arrive with their version of the story : the love-scene between them was a transient aberration in the case of Dolabella and a mere pretence in that of Cleopatra. Antony, of course, does not believe them, and the more they protest, the more is he convinced that there is a plot between them. Here again the situation is good :—

Dol.   If she has wrong'd you,
    Heav'n, hell, and you, revenge it.
Ant.   If she wrong'd me !
    Thou wouldst evade thy part of guilt; but swear
    Thou lov'st not her.
Dol.   Not so as I love you.
Ant. Not so? Swear, swear, I say, thou dost not love her.
Dol. No more than friendship will allow.
Ant.   No more?
    Friendship allows thee nothing ; thou art perjur'd—

And yet thou didst not swear thou lov'dst her not;
But not so much, no more. O trifling hypocrite,
Who dar'st not own to her, thou dost not love,
Nor own to me, thou dost! Ventidius heard it;
Octavia saw it.

Cleo.   They are enemies.
Ant.   Alexas is not so: he, he confess'd it;
He, who, next hell, best knew it, he avow'd it.
(*To Dol.*) Why do I seek a proof beyond yourself?
You, whom I sent to bear my last farewell,
Return'd, to plead her stay.   (491 ff.)

Cleopatra declares that it was she who encouraged
Dolabella in order to make Antony jealous and so
regain him, but Antony still refuses to believe :—

Ant.   Thin cobweb arts of falsehood;
Seen, and broke thro' at first.   (522 f.)

Cleopatra wishes to invoke the testimony of Alexas,
but Antony very naturally depreciates him as the
mere instrument of Cleopatra, and says that he has
told the truth already.   Then regarding himself as
a victim of universal treachery, he bids them go
and, if they have any decency, keep apart. *Exeunt
severally* is the good 'curtain' which concludes this
Act.

Act V

Between Acts IV and V Caesar's fleet attacks the
Egyptian fleet in the harbour of Alexandria, an
arrangement, as afterwards appears, having been
previously made for the surrender of the Egyptians.
The development of events here, *if examined*, is
very obscure, and the 'unity of time' is only vague.

But the exposition would suffice for an audience ;
it is high time for a revolt against Cleopatra.
Antony is watching the action from Pharos (58) ;
he is not fighting—for what reason is not made clear.

The Act opens with Cleopatra and her women.
She threatens suicide, struggles with the women
who prevent her, and upbraids Alexas with his fatal
advice. Alexas still promises to reclaim Antony
and is about to seek him at Pharos, when shouts
are followed by the announcement of the treachery
of the Egyptian fleet. Cleopatra enquires about
Antony ; he is reported almost mad, believing the
treason to be the work of Cleopatra. Alexas offers
to go to Caesar, but this proposal Cleopatra rejects
with scorn, and insists that he shall face Antony
and clear her. Alexas cannot escape ; his extreme
terror of death is expressed with good effect, in a
short soliloquy intervening between the passionate
and rapid scenes before and after :—

> O that I less could fear to lose this being,
> Which, like a snowball in my coward hand,
> The more 'tis grasp'd, the faster melts away.
> Poor reason ! what a wretched aid art thou !
> For still, in spite of thee,
> These two long lovers, soul and body, dread
> Their final separation. Let me think :
> What can I say, to save myself from death ?
> No matter what becomes of Cleopatra.   (131 ff.)

But as his 'gift of lying's gone, and this court
devil,' which he has so often raised, has now forsaken
him, he leaves the scene at the entrance of Antony
and Ventidius.

Antony and Ventidius still have the command of three legions, and agree that they will lose their lives well in a last fight. Then Alexas, trembling, presents himself, and is almost killed on the spot by Ventidius. Antony however interferes : 'he is not worth killing,' but changes his mind on catching what he takes for a hint that Cleopatra has fled to Dolabella :—

> Ingrateful woman!
> Who follow'd me, but as the swallow summer,
> Hatching her young ones in my kindly beams,
> Singing her flatt'ries to my morning wake:
> But, now my winter comes, she spreads her wings,
> And seeks the spring of Cæsar.　　　　　(208 ff.)

Alexas, in agony, flings out a pathetic account of her suicide, to the exultation of Ventidius, but Antony is overwhelmed with grief :—

> Then art thou innocent, my poor dear love?
> And art thou dead?
> O those two words! their sound should be divided:
> Hadst thou been false and died; or hadst thou liv'd,
> And hadst been true.—But innocence and death!
> 　　　　　(256 ff.)

Antony is now resolved to die, and Ventidius refuses to survive him. Antony asks Ventidius to kill him first and then die if he will, and Ventidius deceives Antony, as Eros does in the corresponding scene in *Antony and Cleopatra* (IV 13), by asking him to turn away and then striking himself instead. Antony, after a few farewell words, falls on his sword, but does not die immediately, and as he is

about to make a second attempt, Cleopatra enters
with her women and runs to him :—

Ant.   Art thou living
  Or am I dead before I knew, and thou
  The first kind ghost that meets me?
Cleo.   Help me seat him.
  Send quickly, send for help!
Ant.   I am answer'd.
  We live both. Sit thee down my Cleopatra :
  I'll make the most I can of life, to stay
  A moment more with thee.   (358 ff.)

The whole scene of the farewell is too long **to**
quote ; Antony says they have had their time :
' ten years' love, And, not a moment lost'; Cleopatra
promises to follow quickly, and Antony dies. She
sends her women for 'the aspics ' and, when she is
alone, speaks her farewell :—

  'Tis sweet to die, when they would force life on me ;
  To rush into the dark abode of Death,
  And seize him first ; if he be like my love,
  He is not frightful, sure.
  We're now alone, in secrecy and silence ;
  And is not this like lovers ? I may kiss
  These pale, cold lips ; Octavia does not see me :
  And O ! 'tis better far to have him thus,
  Than see him in her arms.   (442 ff.)

The aspics are brought in, and Cleopatra, after
a momentary recoil, applies one to her arm and is
soon dead. The women, Iras and Charmion, follow
her example. The Egyptians enter with Alexas
bound, and the final tableau is much as in Shakespeare's play, but without the presence of Caesar.

In all this 'the Monument' (as Shakespeare calls the Mausoleum which Cleopatra had built for herself and where she had stored her treasure) is apparently the scene, but the indications are very vague and any interior room in the Palace might serve the purpose.

The general course of the fifth Act is thus quite simple and might be anticipated. It is distinguished by the increased and continuous beauty of the verse, which makes representative selection difficult. Some fine passages have been already quoted, but I must not omit Alexas' description of jealousy when, speaking of Antony and Cleopatra, he says :—

> His heart was never lost, but started off
> To jealousy, love's last retreat and covert;
> Where it lies hid in shades, watchful in silence,
> And list'ning for the sound that calls it back,...
>
> (49 ff.)

nor the lament of Serapion after the treachery of the fleet :—

> Egypt has been, our latest hour is come:
> The queen of nations, from her ancient seat,
> Is sunk for ever in the dark abyss:
> Time has unroll'd her glories to the last,
> And now clos'd up the volume,... (71 ff.)

nor the lines spoken by Antony, after he has learnt of Cleopatra's supposed death, when he abandons the idea of farther resistance :—

Vent. Would you be taken?
Ant.   Yes, I would be taken;
> But, as a Roman ought,—dead, my Ventidius:

For I'll convey my soul from Cæsar's reach,
And lay down life myself. 'Tis time the world
Should have a lord, and know whom to obey.
We two have kept its homage in suspense,
And bent the globe on whose each side we trod,
Till it was dinted inwards. Let him walk
Alone upon 't: I'm weary of my part.
My torch is out; and the world stands before me,
Like a black desart at th' approach of night:
I'll lay me down, and stray no farther on.   (276 ff.)

It remains to consider several critical questions which arise in connexion with Dryden's play. First, and most obvious, comes the comparison with Shakespeare, a comparison inevitable indeed but not much to the purpose. The imperial machinery and its remorseless crushing is visible in the larger scale of *Antony and Cleopatra* but hardly so in *All for Love.* Nor is the character-drawing of Dryden to be compared with that of Shakespeare. Shakespeare's Cleopatra is really unique, unique in the proper sense of the word :—

I saw her once
Hop forty paces through the public street;
And having lost her breath, she spoke, and panted,
That she did make defect perfection,
And, breathless, power breathe forth.
                    (*A. and C.* II 2.)

So speaks Enobarbus, but no such thing is imaginable of Dryden's Cleopatra. With him the whole story is more ordinary; it is dignified but not gigantic. Nor is this the only difference; much more might be said on these lines.

17—2

But there is character-drawing among the lesser personages in *All for Love*, in the futile subtlety of Alexas, in the well-meant blundering of Ventidius, and in the conflict in Dolabella's mind between love and honour, a conflict naturally felt—not conventionally represented, as it had been in *The Conquest of Granada*.

The plot, as I have more than once indicated in the preceding analysis, is well-constructed. Mr Noyes' criticism seems to me very severe. He writes (*Introd.* p. xlix) 'The action, despite its confinement within a single day, is, as Aristotle would call it, "episodic"; like that of *The Conquest of Granada*, it deals with successive adventures in the life of one man, not with a central crisis.' To discuss here[1] what Aristotle calls 'epeisodic' and what he means by 'Unity of Action' would take us too far afield; the essential thing is that the plot 'must imitate one action and that a whole, the structural union of the parts being such that if any one of them is displaced or removed, the whole will be disjointed and disturbed' (Aristotle's *Poetics*, Ch. VIII). In Dryden's play, the sequence of scenes is not perhaps *necessary*, but it is probable, and I do not feel that it can justly be described as 'epeisodic.'

Then we come to Dryden's own objection concerning the introduction of Octavia :—

> The greatest error in the contrivance seems to be in the person of Octavia; for, though I might use the privilege of a poet, to introduce her into Alexandria, yet I had not

[1] See above, p. 127.

enough considered that the compassion she moved to herself and children was destructive to that which I reserved
for Antony and Cleopatra; whose mutual love, being founded
upon vice, must lessen the favour of the audience to them,
when virtue and innocence were oppressed by it. And,
though I justified Antony˙ in some measure, by making
Octavia's departure to proceed wholly from herself; yet the
force of the first machine still remained; and the dividing
of pity, like the cutting of a river into many channels, abated
the strength of the natural stream.

No one, he goes on to say, has urged this objection,
but the author did not choose to be 'partial to'
himself. Dryden likes to take this attitude, which
avoids the appearance of submission. But is the
objection he makes to the introduction of Octavia
well considered? Not all the statements which it
suits him to make can be accepted without demur;
we may, for instance, doubt whether he expresses
his well-considered opinion when he says that he
himself, Shakespeare, and 'the greatest wits of our
nation' were all attracted to the subject of Antony
and Cleopatra by 'the excellency of the moral'—the
misfortunes, that is to say, of vice. Nor is his object
really to concentrate pity on Antony and Cleopatra,
but to show how a long-rooted affection may over-
power every consideration on the other side, so as
to extinguish even regret for the sacrifice—'the
world well lost.' For this purpose Antony's position
must be strong and advantageous; Octavia is part
of this strength and apparently an essential part:
without the introduction of Octavia, the plot must
have been wholly reconstructed. The advantageous

position of Antony at the opening of the play is emphasised : Alexandria is not beleaguered, Ventidius still controls twelve legions, and Caesar, notwithstanding some touches at his 'coldness,' is practically assumed to be quite ready for a family reconciliation through the offices of Octavia.

In the meeting of Octavia and Cleopatra there is certainly no 'French decorum.' This Dryden justifies as follows :—

> The French poets...are strict observers of these punctilios : they would not, for example, have suffered Cleopatra and Octavia to have met; or, if they had met, there must only have passed betwixt them some cold civilities, but no eagerness of repartee, for fear of offending against the greatness of their characters, and the modesty of their sex. This objection I foresaw, and at the same time contemned; for I judged it both natural and probable that Octavia, proud of her new-gained conquest, would search out Cleopatra to triumph over her; and that Cleopatra, thus attacked, was not of a spirit to shun the encounter: and 'tis not unlikely that two exasperated rivals should use such satire as I have put into their mouths; for, after all, though the one were a Roman, and the other a queen, they were both women.

Scott however appears to disagree with Dryden on this point; he writes that Octavia's 'scolding scene with Cleopatra seems too coarse to be in character, and is a glaring exception to the general good taste evinced throughout the rest of the piece.' I must leave the question open for the reader to determine; to me the scene, though conventional, appears not objectionable.

The scene between Antony and Ventidius in

Act I obtained Dryden's own approval : ' I prefer
the scene betwixt Antony and Ventidius in the
first act to anything which I have written in this
kind,' and with this approval the critics have agreed.
The interview represents the triumph of an old
friendship over violent animosity, a hatred really
based in love and passing into it.   The scene between Sebastian and Dorax, in the later play of
Don Sebastian, is somewhat analogous ; it treats of
the revenge of a wronged subject, sought for years,
but abandoned, when the opportunity comes, as
loyalty and honour prevail.   The situation in the
scene between Antony and Ventidius suits Dryden's
powers, and there is no necessity for fine touches,
which were not his forte.

Finally let us set side by side for comparison
the description of the barge on Cydnus, in the plays
of Shakespeare and of Dryden.

All for Love, Act III 60 ff.

Antony is recalling the scene to Dolabella :—

Ant.   To clear herself,
    For sending him no aid, she came from Egypt.
    Her galley down the silver Cydnos row'd,
    The tackling silk, the streamers wav'd with gold ;
    The gentle winds were lodg'd in purple sails :
    Her nymphs, like Nereids, round her couch were plac'd,
    Where she, another sea-born Venus, lay.
Dol.   No more ; I would not hear it.
Ant.   O, you must !
    She lay, and leant her cheek upon her hand,
    And cast a look so languishingly sweet,

As if, secure of all beholders' hearts,
Neglecting she could take 'em: boys, like Cupids,
Stood fanning with their painted wings the winds
That play'd about her face: but if she smil'd,
A darting glory seem'd to blaze abroad,
That men's desiring eyes were never wearied,
But hung upon the object. To soft flutes
The silver oars kept time; and while they play'd,
The hearing gave new pleasure to the sight;
And both to thought. 'Twas heav'n, or somewhat more:
For she so charm'd all hearts that gazing crowds
Stood panting on the shore and wanted breath
To give their welcome voice.

Antony and Cleopatra, Act II Scene 2.

Enobarbus is describing the scene to Agrippa:—

Eno.   I will tell you.
The barge she sat in, like a burnish'd throne,
Burn'd on the water: the poop was beaten gold;
Purple the sails, and so perfumed that
The winds were love-sick with them: the oars were silver,
Which to the tune of flutes kept stroke and made
The water which they beat to follow faster,
As amorous of their strokes. For her own person,
It beggar'd all description: she did lie
In her pavilion, cloth-of-gold of tissue,
O'er-picturing that Venus where we see
The fancy outwork nature: on each side her
Stood pretty dimpled boys, like smiling Cupids,
With divers-colour'd fans, whose wind did seem
To glow the delicate cheeks which they did cool,
And what they undid did.
Agr.   O, rare for Antony!
Eno. Her gentlewomen, like the Nereides,
So many mermaids, tended her i' the eyes,

And made their bends adornings: at the helm
A seeming mermaid steers: the silken tackle
Swell with the touches of those flower-soft hands,
That yarely frame the office. From the barge
A strange invisible perfume hits the sense
Of the adjacent wharfs. The city cast
Her people out upon her; and Antony,
Enthron'd i' the market place, did sit alone,
Whistling to the air; which, but for vacancy,
Had gone to gaze on Cleopatra too,
And made a gap in Nature.

In comparing the passages we must remember who is the speaker in each case; Enobarbus is a more impressive witness than Antony, to whom Dryden has transferred the description.

Is either passage a very good specimen of its author? Certainly neither is above criticism. Thus in Shakespeare's lines we may take exception to the oars which make the water follow faster '*as amorous of their strokes*'; and to the air which 'but for vacancy, Had gone to gaze on Cleopatra too, And made a gap in Nature'! I am glad also to be rid of 'yarely frame the office' and of 'did seem,' 'did cool,' 'what they undid did.' But on the other hand we miss the barge 'burn'd on the water'—her person 'beggar'd all description'—'tended her i' the eyes'—and the 'invisible perfume.' These touches Dryden seems to have dropped needlessly.

Scott, who compares the two passages, prefers Dryden for 'the easy flow of the verse, which seems to soften with the subject,' and for the rapture 'without hyperbole.' As to the first point, the softening of the verse with its subject, it should be remembered that Enobarbus is not a lover, whereas Antony is, and so the difference may be justified.

The reader has before him the material for forming a judgement, and I will leave the subject—only noting the characteristic touch in Dryden's description, ''twas heav'n, *or somewhat more.*'

INDEX